WHAT

KIND OF

LIFE

Jon Thum

Published by What Kind Of Books
First published 2015

Printed by Createspace
1

Although this book is a true account,
some names have been changed
to protect the privacy of individuals

For a photographic accompaniment,
and further information, please visit:

www.jonthum.com

for

Sil, Zuri and Leon

with love and respect to

Leo

introduction

Call me what you will: observer, judge, philosopher, or just plain commentator; I am all of these, yet somehow there is more to it ..... a connection, an empathy, yes.

For that is my role in this story of a life.

And inasmuch as you, the reader, will form your own opinions, I shall likewise declare my hand. For although I cannot be the ticking heart of this book - that can only be the subject himself - I will try in the same spirit to be its inner voice, its moral conscience if you like: a battler and conqueror of demons.

What kind of life? What kind of life!
Both punctuations can hope to be used ...

For what makes a man take the path he does in life with his short time in the world? How can we say when those dark forces that drive us, hidden from conscious thought, should be judged with merit or otherwise? Well, there are clues to be found, and these I will present to you with the humblest objectivity I can muster.

For what follows is a true account that will bear no embellishments or alterations of facts; that is, beyond a man's natural ability to remember things that have long ago passed. There will be great journeys, five in all, a tipping point, a settling, and then a twist of sorts.

Is there an ending? Yes, in a manner of speaking there is; if there could ever be one fork in the road to place a full stop, then this is surely it. A happy one? Perhaps, and this is one for the reader to judge, not I. It is at the very least unexpected, and like so many endings, one that will mark the start of yet another episode ...

PART 1

1. going home

I am staring out of the window in a mild hash-infused haze at the Chinese countryside which is passing like scenery cards, near then far, through our narrow frame to the world. The train seems to be climbing, and the pace is slow, rickety. We pass through a long dark tunnel and suddenly there it is, unexpected and at once exhilarating. The sun is low, yet unmistakably picks out the broken edge of a long stone wall.

"It's the fucking wall!"

We shout almost in unison, for we are both transfixed by the view. Kurt, with a flourish, reaches for our tape collection and produces .... of course, Pink Floyd: The Wall, which is hastily rewound to the title track on our ghetto-blaster. What follows is both sublime and surreal. For two hours, the train zigzags back and forth amongst the ruins of the Great Wall of China in perfect timing to a setting sun, in and out of the hills so we see it here then there, always mounting a crest then descending beyond. This impromptu show feels like it's played out in slow motion, intensified as it is by our tripped out state, and I can see in Kurt's eyes the same crazy wonder that must be reflected in mine. When we finally bid farewell, the wall is just a silhouette casting a thin black line across the hills.

It is in fact something of a happy accident that we are high, for shortly after leaving Beijing, and with no idea of what was to come, we sensibly decided to finish the remains of our stash in anticipation of reaching the Mongolian border later in the day. After waiting for the attendant to finish his ticket inspection and retire to his quarters, we had stood cautiously in the open doorway at the end of the carriage, smoking our joints disguised as cigarettes. And once this surreptitious disposal of the evidence was complete, so to speak, we could finally relax and enjoy the journey ...

It's the summer of 1988, and we have just boarded the Trans-Siberian express. Perhaps the word 'express' is misleading, for this will be a ten day journey broken only by a short stay in Moscow, and will take in China, Mongolia, Russia, Poland and East Germany on the way to our destination - Berlin.

We are on our way home.

I have been travelling for fifteen months, Kurt for two years. Both in our mid twenties, we met over a year ago completely by chance in a bar in Bangkok - Kurt looking for someone to share a bottle of Mekong whisky with, and I at once a willing accomplice.

He: an ex-dealer from Amsterdam, his six foot frame taut with lean muscle and topped by blue-grey eyes, five o'clock shadow and curly mop tied in a ponytail. With semi-sunken eyes, there is something to suggest a junkie past; but like the owner of a look-alike dog, it's hard to say whether his face fits the profile or the other way round. And I: six foot three, skinny and blue-eyed, two piercings in one ear and short spiky hair, a throwback to the late seventies of my teens. That late night drink in the Khaosan Road was the start of a long and lasting friendship, a bond that grew strong from both the intense shared experience of travelling together and what became a crazy amalgamation of both our sense of humours.

But now is a time for reminiscing, and there is a hint of sadness in the air; our journey is about to end. In Beijing, we have been busy preparing for this trip home with almost military precision. Here is a page from my diary that Kurt dictated to me one day:

Tomorrow, the 15th May, we, that is Jon and Kurt wake up at 8.00 a.m. precisely.

At 8.30 a.m. they will be on their way by means of bicycle (rented) towards the C.I.T.S. (China International Travel Service).

They will find their way by means of Sergeant Scout Jon (an experienced orienteer).

On arrival at the C.I.T.S they will make sure that their bicycles are safely secured.

After entering they will be utmost kind towards the person dealing with the reservation of their ticket.

THE TARGET - Wednesday 25th May, the Chinese train.

If this is not possible we will, if necessary, use violence.

If this is not effective, we will book the earliest possible train out of Beijing.

Afterwards we will hold a meeting (wherever) with the results of the two answers. *This will decide the way of approaching the Polish guy to get our ticket as soon as possible.*

The Polish guy is in fact the reason we are here at all. He and a small group of associates operate a business out of a travellers hotel in Beijing. It's a story we've heard on the grapevine, and it's been reinforced often enough for us to take the risk in coming here. This is how it works: he buys up as many return tickets as he can from his home town in Poland, and armed with these - and his own ticket of course - he sets off on the long journey to Beijing. The subsidised price of these tickets in Poland is negligible compared to the tourist prices set by the government in Beijing, and because the return portion is left open, this part can be sold on to a traveller and rebooked at the aforementioned CITS, the government ticket agency. The outward half of the ticket is thrown away. There are two trains every week for the traveller to choose from, and each takes a different route; we prefer the Chinese train which travels through Mongolia, rather than the Russian train which passes around it. The going price for one of these black market tickets is 80 U.S. dollars, a fraction of the cost of a flight, and with the added value of a Trans-Siberian adventure thrown in, it's an opportunity that can't be missed. For this reason alone, we've taken a big detour from Thailand to come here, taking in the Philippines and Hong Kong en route.

We locate the Polish guy in the lobby of our hotel with huge relief; it is in fact the only travellers hotel in Beijing, and everyone seems to be here for the same reason. He sits quietly going about his business on one of the plush sofas, as his potential customers stand furtively in the background awaiting their turn. It's a curious building, built in the Soviet style and set alongside a canal and a field that look almost rural in outlook. Holed up here are the few white faces to be seen around Beijing, apart from the whistle stop buses that turn up in the more touristic sites now and again - Tiananman Square and the like.

And next door to the hotel is the restaurant where we eat most of our meals. It's formal in presentation - a navy blue carpet, and tables laid carefully with two white table cloths, serviettes and stainless steel chopsticks - with a lengthy menu and waiter service. And it is here that we are taught some important cultural lessons.

The Chinese, who come from outside of the hotel, are loud and rude. They shout to the waiters across the room and pick at their food, dropping unwanted morsels casually onto the floor. At first we are a bit disgusted, but after a while we decide to do as the locals do. My dish is full of gristle, and most of it ends up on the floor behind me - it feels appropriate and strangely satisfying.

And there are Americans here too; one evening, we are stuck on a table with two young couples, and they are not happy. The women complain that there are no public toilets in Beijing, presumably having been caught short earlier in the day. Then, as they peruse the Chinese menu, the conversation between them goes like this:

"I really miss the food back home."

"I like Pizza."

"Yeah! Which one? I like Pizza Hut."

"I like Domino's."

"Yeah, wow! I could really eat Domino's now."

Kurt says: "For fuck's sake you're in China."

There are in fact a number of missions we need to complete here in our mock-military-style, apart from securing those cheap train tickets. Visas are required for Mongolia, Russia and Poland, and thus the tortuous queuing and filling in of forms to get our stamps of approval from various far-flung parts of the city. We will have to visit them twice, once for drop off and once for collection. And this of course requires transport, for which the budget minded is left with only one choice - the bicycle.

At this time in Beijing, bicycles are an overwhelming presence; the streets are thick with them, and all manner of car-related issues apply to them too: traffic jams, disputes, collisions, road rage. Roundabouts are particularly perilous, with no discernible rules as to who goes first, and we find ourselves weaving this way and that, sometimes missing our turn. And not unnaturally, being amateurs at this game, we find ourselves one day in an accidental collision with one of the locals, slamming hard into his rear wheel as he cuts across us. With me riding pillion and Kurt pedalling - since to hire one bike instead of two will buy us an extra beer in the evening - we are pursued down the road by this angry Chinaman, who kicks at our wheels in an attempt to knock us over. At first we are a little thrown by this act of aggression, but after a while I kick back, more in defence than anything else, while Kurt curses loudly in Dutch: "Kut! Godverdomme!" More insults are exchanged, though not understood by either party, and after several kicks he seems satisfied and is on his way. This display causes much amusement to the surrounding public who point and laugh energetically; it's something we've witnessed before in China - when a fight breaks out or a dog is viciously kicked, the reaction of onlookers is largely one of hilarity rather than concern. It's a disconcerting reaction.

And while we are out negotiating the hazards of these busy streets, we also need to stock up on provisions for our trip. So far, buying things in China has rarely been straightforward, and we believe this to be related to a number of issues. First, there are two currencies in circulation - the local yuan and the tourist yuan, two different sets of notes with the same face value. The tourist yuan (known as Foreign Exchange Certificates) is the one exchanged in banks, and its rate is fixed by the government; these can then in turn be swapped on the streets for local yuan at the black market rate, almost two for the price of one. So we maintain two sets of currencies and pay with the local one whenever possible. When any particular trader is confronted by a foreigner offering local currency for his wares, his inclination is to hold out for payment with tourist yuan where there is a clear profit to be made. Alternatively his motive may be noble, for we are not officially allowed to have local yuan at all. Nonetheless, the result is the same, and there is no sale. We move on to a different shop.

But on some occasions this explanation is not sufficient. In many places we are simply ignored, and the money is not even seen leaving our wallets. In one shop we point furiously at the racks of cigarettes in a nicotine-starved panic, while miming the act of inhalation and exhalation with two fingers to our lips. The shop keeper does not even meet our eyes. And many a time in restaurants we have had to leave after a period of futile waiting, watching all and sundry being served around us while our stomachs rumble enviously at the food on display. The theory we have heard to account for this behaviour is a deep routed mistrust of foreigners, which is framed in some historical context such as the opium wars. Suffice to say that the word they use for foreign visitors is a literal translation of the word 'barbarian'.

With perseverance though, and this being Beijing where perhaps the more enlightened Chinese reside, we manage to stock up on the staples for our trip: beer, cigarettes, batteries, tea, and a rather uninspiring selection of tinned meats and crackers. Most of the tins we buy are completely unfathomable to us apart from a small picture to represent its contents, so we are particularly pleased when we find one that we recognise: alongside the Chinese symbols on the side, this one says in plain English - Peking Duck. This motley collection of tins with their mysterious contents could have been catastrophically unappetising were it not for our trump card: Filipino sweet chilli sauce. This magical substance we discovered in the Philippines, a country where bland food prevailed, and one particularly good brand of sauce came to the rescue. Armed with two bottles of these, there would be nothing that could faze us, not even dog food; the chances of us having bought this by accident are slim, however - the Chinese tend to eat their dogs rather than feed them.

The imported items for our trip are no less important. Vodka, bought duty free on the Hong Kong to Guangzhou ferry - two bottles. Valium, bought in Bangkok (we have considered the fact that we may get bored on such a long train journey) - forty tablets. Also from Bangkok - denim and music tapes to sell for roubles in Russia (the official exchange rate there is also artificially high), though I am doubtful that the cheap unfashionable jeans that Kurt has bought could be desired by anyone, anywhere; we will see ...

And souvenirs - we can carry more luggage now that we are on our way home. For some reason we are taken with the local art. There are sellers crouched by the roadside near the hotel who, in clandestine fashion, unroll their works of art before you as you pass. Always watercolours with bold strokes on thin rice paper, but with different subjects - a Samurai warrior, a Chinese garden, a plain Chinese symbol with some spiritual meaning. They are so cheap, we buy them up enthusiastically; unfortunately we do not consider that they will be viewed differently through more discerning eyes, and thus are unaware of their true destiny - unwanted gifts left in the cupboards and attics of our extended families back home.

Then amongst all this preparation and day to day existence, a shock. I am in the hotel room, rolling up my latest works of art into a neat tube, when Kurt comes in. His face is ashen, and if it weren't for my lack of superstition in this regard, I would say he had actually seen a ghost. More likely, something really bad has happened.

"Jon, sit down," he says.

"Why? What happened?" my mind is spinning with all the possibilities, but nothing is registering yet.

"There's someone downstairs in the lobby. You won't believe it."

"Who?" and this time another spin, but still no click of the wheel to register a name.

"It's Stacey."

It was then that I sat down.

2. sydney

And now a flood of memories; never mind that the wheel has clicked, there is now a whole torrent let loose through those sluice gates. For although they were happy times, the best it may be said, there are reasons why they have been quietly locked away and stored in safe keeping for another time ...

It is August of 87, and Kurt and I have just arrived in Sydney, ostensibly to earn more cash for our travels. I have no real expectation of what Sydney will be like, and after we are dispensed from the airport bus at Central Station, I am a little taken aback by its American style high-rise business district with its efficient metro and bus system - even a monorail is under construction. It is a modern businesslike city at first glance and, unlike the stereotypical Aussie persona, one that takes itself seriously. It is in stark contrast to the jungle and beaches of Thailand where we have just come from; but we are here to work, and we are determined.

Having found lodgings at The Pink House, a dormitory style hostel so named for obvious reasons, we start our job search the following morning at 6 a.m. The mornings are cold, for it is winter here and we do not have any warm clothes of any note, our bags having been packed for tropical climes. We queue patiently, shifting from foot to foot to keep warm, until let in quietly through a side door to the job centre at 6.30 a.m.

"Any panel beaters here?" a voice calls out.

We sit at the back of a large room, awaiting our turn. If we stay until 9.30, our names will go onto a list; those at the top of the list will be offered the next unskilled job. We are straight in the charts at number 85 and 86.

"Any sandwich makers here?" he booms again.

For a moment I am filled with hope: surely we can make a sandwich? I hesitate, my arm half raised.

"Six months experience," he qualifies, and all raised hands are lowered in unison.

And so we repeat this daily routine for four days, until finally we enter the top ten. Jobs are being handed out regularly now - a building site labourer here, a gardener there - and we await our fate with some trepidation, until the countdown on our fingers is empty ...

Suddenly, both our names are read out along with another - three jobs at once! It's the best result we could have possibly hoped for; Kurt and I will present ourselves for work at a handbag warehouse in Redfern tomorrow, our short term fates loosely entwined once again ...

We prove ourselves to be hard and enthusiastic workers, eager to impress; handbags, rucksacks and wallets are retrieved from the aisles at lightning speed, packed in boxes with the utmost vigour, and orders are dispatched in record time. Our boss takes us aside after a few days.

"Slow down, mate. Not so fast okay? There's plenty of time." He mumbles something about the unions, and we get it; we flash a smile to each other, and we slow down.

Now a new routine takes shape. The early rise and walk to the metro through the main drag of Kings Cross, with the spent energy of the night before still lingering: strip clubs, slot machines, sex shops, most are closed now, but the odd one ejects a late reveller. Then my favourite moment, as the train exits the Kings Cross tunnel and emerges high over the city on a sweeping viaduct. A sudden flash reveals the Sydney skyline still submerged in the shadows of the morning light, and like this we are welcomed into the day.

The work has become easier at the warehouse now, and a social life soon emerges; our fellow workers are mostly travellers themselves, from Ireland, Germany and New Zealand. We save money by bringing sandwiches for lunch (we are now experts in this field) and by cooking our own dinners: 'chibichi' is one such speciality - cheesy beans, made with curried fried onions and served with thin sliced chips. We name it as you would a new invention. On some nights we eat at the Hare Krishna restaurant, where free meals are served in a back street to those who bring their own empty plates; the clientele is a mixture of homeless and travellers who have hit hard times, but the food is sensationally good. And at weekends, we buy a case of beer straight from the cold room of our local bottle shop to celebrate. The bottle tops are saved to become the pieces for our backgammon board, which we have drawn onto a large piece of plywood. Swan Lager will be the whites, Victoria Bitter the reds.

A few weeks later, we get another break. Kurt has secured us an apartment which we will share and sublet from Gunner, a Swedish friend of his. The apartment building is close by, and from its modest four level facade on Victoria Street, it backs onto the side of an escarpment where it sinks a further six floors to the street below. We have a partial view of the city skyline, which can be seen from one corner of the living room where a chair is strategically placed. It is more than enough for us. Kurt shares the bedroom with Gunner, and I opt for the living room floor. There are several notes left around the building from its Nazi-style landlord, and as we descend in the lift we read this one:

'*To the low life cretin who spits in this lift: when I find you, I'm gonna rip off your head and spit down your throat - then I'm gonna evict you.*'

And the streets around here really do seem paved with gold. On several occasions we find banknotes on the pavement, slipped from the grasp of a fumbling drunk. Then one day we find the unwanted contents of a recently evacuated house along the street, left generously for someone to stumble upon. Amongst the crates there is a record collection, some lamps, two avant-garde paintings and five box-loads of books - a collection of classics so complete, that it must have been garnered from a lifelong passion of reading. We will come to love some of these books, and one in particular will become resonant to our stay - Tortilla Flat by John Steinbeck. For like the paisanos of that book who are drawn together under one roof to become something bigger than their constituent parts, so our apartment too will soon bring together a similar happy band of renegades ...

On one providential night, we are drinking in our local, the Rex Hotel. It has an eclectic crowd, a mix of travellers and locals, and Kurt and I are prone to circulating the room when drunk, introducing ourselves to strangers. This time though, we are seated, and spot a girl across the room who is engaged in energetic conversation with a small group. There is something about her we are both drawn to: pretty, in a sexy, understated way, with matching brown eyes and hair, she is dressed smartly in work-like skirt and heels, but her manner and eyes betray something far less straight-laced and formal than her clothes would suggest. In short, there is a hint of danger that lures us in.

Kurt is the bolder of us, and in minutes he is there talking to her and inviting her to our table. Without almost a second thought, she gets up and, eyes locked into mine, she crosses the room to join us.

And that is how Stacey walked into our lives, crazy and wasted that night in a way that would soon become familiar to us: outspoken and challenging, but at the same time funny and completely left of field, with a mischievous giggle that leaves you bewitched. There is an overwhelming joy in this discovery, in the way that you feel when you unexpectedly unlock someone's plain facade to find a wickedly comical view of the world. It turns out that she's from Hackney, and is on some kind of 'last gasp of freedom' trip before she returns to marry her boyfriend. She is working as a secretary somewhere in the business district to support her somewhat Jekyll and Hyde lifestyle.

And after Stacey, we are soon introduced to Gavin, an English language teacher she has met along the way. Tall, blonde, and dressed in denim suit, he often turns up at our apartment unannounced on a small child's bicycle he found abandoned in the street, legs bent sideways and knees to shoulders, pedalling furiously. These two would soon become part of our informal gang; there is not one particular moment when you could say that this happened but, just as in spring you wake one day to find that summer has arrived, so it was with them ...

The four of us become adept at finding parties. In preparation for our evening out, we first get stoned, this being Kurt the Dutchman's well established custom to make the drink last longer. Then we head off into the night, usually following a tip about a Swedish party somewhere, or just walk the streets until we find one; Kings Cross is full of Swedes hellbent on getting drunk, a pastime that's prohibitively expensive in their own country. We enter with beer cans generously on display, then leave with them tucked under our shirts ready for the next party. On the way home, Gavin and I often indulge in our habit of serenading strangers, something that began quite spontaneously. He has been learning to play the blues harp, and often blows the only four-note phrase he knows, a classic blues riff. His chorus is simply one long blow on a vibrating note. One day I decide to sing along on the bus:

> *wah waaaah wah wah!* ... "hey you over there"
> *wah waaaah wah wah!* ... "I'm talkin' 'bout you"
> *wah waaaah wah wah!* ... "you been out somewhere"
> *wah waaaah wah wah!* ... "and you're feeling kinda blue!"
> *wah waaaah wah wah!* ... "I'm talkin' 'bout you"
> *wah waaaah wah wah!* ... "the girl with the hair"
> *wah waaaah wah wah!* ... "you're looking for love"
> *wah waaaah wah wah!* ... "and you're going nowhere!"
> *waaauwaauwaaa!*

Most of the time I manage to make up something that rhymes, and after some practice we become quite proficient; on one occasion, the whole metro carriage breaks into spontaneous applause as we leave the train. We should have passed a hat.

On some nights we take speed, and this usually requires a visit to a famous night spot, the Taxi Club, which is the only place we know that's open after 2 a.m. It looks more like a casino than a disco, for although there is a dance floor at the back, its rooms are full of slot machines, and dispersed amongst these are its regular residents - the transvestites. They are nothing like I have seen before: burly and tattooed, unshaven and broken-toothed, with their large overflowing package usually squeezed into a skimpy sequinned dress with heels. For us it's a suitably bizarre place to end the evening.

Then on Sundays we have a special place to go to nurse our hangovers. The best Dutch cure being an early joint of course, we take a bus afterwards to the Bondi Hotel, where we sit on the terrace in the sun sipping beer as the breeze rolls in from the sea. There is always a resident band there, and they play 'Sitting on the dock of the bay' and 'He ain't heavy, He's my brother' amongst other laid back blues. It's a moment of bliss, and we all sit lost in our own thoughts, quietly soaking up the atmosphere.

And soon there are more hangers on to our group - Pai, a Maori built like a brick shithouse, who often comes by to see us, on one occasion nursing a broken arm after one of his frequent drunken blackouts:

"What happened?" I ask.

"Oh, I fell through a plate glass window."

"How the fuck did that happen?"

"Don't really remember, er, guess I was in a fight or something."

Pai is our loose connection to the underworld, an ex-bouncer, and it's always interesting to hear his stories, although we never can work out what he actually does. He has the sweetest disposition you can imagine, but you wouldn't ever want to see his dark side.

There are many others who drop by unexpectedly like this; we have been liberally passing on our address to all and sundry. No one has a phone, and our place becomes a drop-in centre for all sorts - Gavin's Japanese students, our own handbag warehouse colleagues, drinking acquaintances, all are welcome.

And on occasion a Swedish girl, Anna, who I met on one of those long nights out at the Rex, knocks on the door. She always arrives late at night unannounced, presumably at the end of her waitressing shift. We never talk; she comes just to have sex and leave. Of course I don't mind this apparent gender reversal, in fact I'm somewhat flattered, and make no complaints about being woken up in the middle of the night. It ends suddenly though, when Gavin, unaware of our connection, insults her in the pub one night and I neglect to intervene, my allegiances temporarily thrown. Perhaps by then it had run its course anyway.

One of the last to join us is Stuart, a young Aussie from Newcastle, stocky and strong, slightly in awe of us, and eager to please. Importantly he has the use of his girlfriend's car, and this we use to great effect when jumping from one party to another. One weekend we are invited to his father's ranch where, amongst other things, we hope to get a sight of kangaroos. When we finally find a small group, he pulls out a rifle.

"No, don't shoot them!"

"Seriously? They're vermin," he informs us.

"Just not today, okay?" I implore, and he reluctantly puts the rifle back in the car.

This is one of our rare excursions beyond the suburbs of Sydney, and soon there will be another. The Sydney Morning Herald has announced on its front page the devastating news of a marijuana drought in Sydney. All of our regular suppliers have run out, but Stuart interestingly has a lead.

So we all travel up to Newcastle crammed into the car, and in the dead of night a deal is done at a nondescript address in the centre of town, its streets eerily deserted like a well worn cliché. Stuart returns to the car with a large package wrapped in foil. He nods to us in confidence, but we are wary of being ripped off and open the package anxiously; inside is a half kilo brick of compressed Thai stick, something of a delicacy in these parts. We are overjoyed.

And this must be close to the apex now for this particular band of renegades. Summer is arriving, and we are flush with Thai stick, the rest of Sydney cruelly starved of their favourite crop. At the same time, like Pilon and Danny from the hills of Tortilla Flat, Kurt and I, with our ragbag group of friends, are gaining momentum like a stone gathering moss. For we have it all now: our freedom, our health, money to do what we want, the best of friends to enjoy it with, and all in a beautiful city that's blossoming into summer; we are rich with the best things that life has to offer, and almost without a care in the world.

Then suddenly we get some time off work to enjoy this all the more. A strike is called by the unions, and we are sent home until the matter is resolved the following week. We spend this spare time on the beach, in the parks and on the roof of our block with its stunning views of the harbour. There is something special about this city, its natural beauty and hot summer, that gives you the feeling you are endlessly on holiday. It is now, officially, my favourite place to be in the world.

In the background, however, there is a clock counting down on this paradise - tick-tock tick-tock - because although firmly locked away in the back of our minds for now, Kurt and I are moving slowly but inexorably through the second half of our six month work visa.

One day we find a note from Gunner on the table. It is not the first. We have been waging a war of notes lately: Gunner with a '*Hey guys, can you clean up the kitchen sometimes so I can eat please.*' We reply with a lengthy page listing how we would prefer to be asked in person, and how we don't wish to be addressed as 'guys' either, King Kurt and Sir Jon being our preferred terms of address. This latest one is more serious though - he has had enough and is moving out.

And from that note flows a quick chain of events. We need someone to take on the responsibility of a new lease, and Stuart bravely steps up. But at the same time there is someone else looking for a place to stay, and we all agree to loan out the sofa. Our fourth and very welcome new member of the household is Stacey.

3. paradise lost

There are cockroaches in the kitchen, a vast colony, and it's on our food. Not the big ones, but the smaller German variety I am told. We arm ourselves with large cans of insecticide and pounce; all at once every corner of the kitchen is sprayed, but something goes wrong. They are not dying like they're supposed to, but running through our legs and out of the kitchen. We turn in horror to see them spread out in all directions across the living room; there are thousands of them, and the carpet appears to be moving. We give chase and spray recklessly, but it is too late; they are everywhere.

From now on, I will wake every morning to find my bedside glass of water filled with drowned roaches, the odd one still struggling hopelessly. But I am quickly accustomed to this mostly harmless infestation, and thankfully there will be no more plagues like this to visit us. The only disease yet to come will be entirely in my head ...

Christmas is approaching, and an unexpected gift arrives. I am working in the delivery bay at the warehouse, and amongst the arrivals that day is a box that does not belong. It is full of T-shirts instead of the usual bags or wallets, and is clearly destined for some fashion boutique or other. After a quick consultation with Kurt, the box is hidden away carefully in the warehouse. The problem for us now is how to get it out.

We have already been taught by the permanent staff how to pilfer bags from the warehouse if you so desire. It's quite simple: when you are working in the delivery bay, you mark a delivery as one short and its stock count is recorded thus; you can then remove the item later at your leisure. One piece here and there doesn't cause a stir. The difficulty for us now is that an unknown member of staff is stealing wallets without adjusting the stock, and the management is on the alert; we are all now inspected as we leave in the evening for any unusual padding in our attire.

And so a plan is made, and a military style operation ensues. T-shirts are crammed into a sports bag, the bag hidden amongst empty boxes, and these in turn taken to the skip for disposal. We leave work as normal but return at two in the morning, adrenalin pumping, to remove the bag from the skip. If we had worn black and balaclavas, it would not have felt out of place.

The T-shirts prove to be quite fashionable and better than your ordinary fare. We wear some ourselves and sell a few of them, mostly to women. At the same time we are off-loading some of our grass stash, making money back on our investment by selling small foils to our work colleagues. Curiously to us, the buyers are predominantly middle aged and married; smoking grass appears to be as much of an Australian pastime as one arm bandits and the amber nectar.

But there is something about this Thai stick that makes people want more. Yes, it gives you a feeling of euphoria, a heightening of the senses, and often an infectious laughter; but there is something else that sets it apart. This batch is categorically and unquestionably a monstrous aphrodisiac. And as the bong is passed round our flat from time to time, it is of course Stacey that is always there with us; sultry, provocative, irresistible Stacey.

Then all of a sudden, there is a change of temperature between the two of us. One late night we are being thrown out of a Swedish party by the male hosts, not unnaturally because the party is over, but Stacey has started an argument with one of them. She is pushed into a wall aggressively, and I am suddenly like a bull to a red rag; in the ensuing struggle, I find myself travelling down the stairs head first with two Swedes attached. One of them breaks my fall to a degree, but I am still left with burn marks on my arms. To my surprise, Stacey is a little enamoured by this somewhat foolish, yet chivalrous, display.

Another party soon comes along, but this time an invisible barrier is breached between us. Like magnets whose poles are haplessly opposed, a sudden twist of this unstable state and ... snap ... we are slammed together. There is a frenzy of kissing and groping, a breast is revealed, fellatio is simulated with clothes intact; in short, all that could possibly be achieved without the privacy of one's own room. It's like a storm unleashed, and this one rages on until all those pent-up energies are well and truly spent. Yet despite the haze of cocktails through which this act has been performed, I am conscious of something meaningful. I feel like I am in love.

The next day on the Bondi Hotel terrace, the band is on a break, and Kurt has just gone to buy another round. There's a beat, before Stacey says sheepishly:

"Why haven't you said anything?"

"Do you want to talk?" I say. The air has been uncertain, and I, like her maybe, am unsure of my footing.

"I don't know, I mean, I'm getting married ...."

There's a long pause, I am thinking.

"There's not much I can say to that," I conclude.

It is not, however, the end of our tryst. We are now sharing the same room of our apartment, and it's not long before the weed casts its spell on us once more. This time, those conflicting emotions in Stacey's head are more conspicuous. Clothes removed this time, we kiss passionately, then abruptly I am slapped across the face three times, quite hard. A hesitation ... and suddenly we are snapped back together in embrace again. The pattern repeats. There is penetration, but that too is cut short with a shove; finally she starts crying and it's all over. To my despair, it feels that in this moment I have lost the battle.

It is at the very end of Tortilla Flat that Danny goes mad, and this will be the last parallel that I will draw from that particular story. The reasons for my madness are not like Danny's; his angry rejection of the burden of responsibility is quite the opposite to mine, for here I am the object of rejection by another party. The result, however, will share the same sorry fate: the break up of the group.

For now I become slowly consumed by jealousy. This most unwelcome visitor is quiet at first, speaking only in whispers, but it's voice will demand to be heard. At first everything is calm, and Stacey and I revert to our previous platonic state - a stand has been made, a mark put in the sand, and it will be respected.

But soon there is something new developing right before my eyes.

There is a growing closeness now between Kurt and Stacey, a flirtation even. And with this, a switch is flipped in my head, and a neon sign is flashing: .. I .. Have .. To .. Get .. Out.

And so I escape the flat as often as I can. I spend the days in the parks brooding, and in the evenings I drink. On one occasion, two Australians at the Rex are exposed to my ill temper. They are goading me with that tedious playground humour that is popular in this country. They do not relent, and I suddenly explode, pushing one then the other onto opposite tables. They are left almost comically sprawling. The Maori bouncers arrive quickly and remove them both from the pub, while I am left standing calmly, beer still in hand. Somewhat elated by this lucky escape, I bask in the adrenaline rush for the rest of the evening; but it is only a temporary respite.

For each time now that I try to escape, I am getting more and more wasted. During one self-destructive episode, I out-drink and out-smoke everyone in the room until they have all dropped like flies. My madness feels complete, and in the night I suffer a fit. Waking up with an electric jolt to the head, I listen to myself mumbling and stuttering out of control for over a minute, like an extended short circuit of the brain, until I am mercifully returned to normal. The experience is petrifying; I have been suitably warned ...

This unhappy state of affairs cannot last, and the day of confrontation and resolution is soon upon us. There is a party at our flat, and I find solace in kissing a girl, but I am not kidding myself or her that this is anything meaningful. There is a good atmosphere, but Kurt and Stacey are close again. With drink coursing through my veins, there is a spark that sets me off - perhaps a touch by her on him, or him on her. Outside the flat I punch a hole clean through a reinforced glass window; like a snapshot, a perfect circle of glass fragments hurtling through the void, frozen in time and space, is etched into my mind. The noise has easily pierced through the music of the party, and as I sit trying to calm down at the top of the stairs, Kurt arrives threatening with a stick.

"What the fuck is wrong with you?"

"WHAT THE FUCK IS WRONG WITH YOU!" he repeats.

"I CAN'T STAY HERE ANYMORE!" I shout back.

"It's Stacey, I have to fucking leave."

The next few weeks are much calmer. Kurt and I have booked our flight back to Singapore and discarded plans to travel around Australia. It would have been nearly impossible to extend our work visas, and our money will go a lot further in South East Asia. We have both tacitly acknowledged the developing rift as a catalyst for this move, but we bear no malice; this particular one was entirely of my own imagining, and our friendship is far stronger. And with that die cast, there is much planning to be done: bank accounts must be emptied, visas acquired, bags must be packed. And arrangements must be made for one final send off ...

On the morning of our departure, I awake in a daze. For a moment I am lost, but then I piece together in reverse the events of the night before. There is a pain in my crotch, and a quick inspection reveals a nasty looking burn; there is actual skin missing.

A clue ...

The friction ... of course! I was on the roof with a girl, a brunette; and Kurt, he was with a redhead in the flat. Their names ... Jill ... Sally ... both Kiwis. I can hardly believe it; we both scored on the same night, a feat of astonishing unlikelihood.

But there are further surprises; my wallet is stuffed full of twenty dollar notes. Really stuffed ...

The books! I remember now; we sold our collection to a bookshop in the afternoon. But still that doesn't explain ...

The T-shirts! Yes, we sold them all to an Israeli traveller last night; about a hundred were left at last count.

And while there are still events from the previous evening that cannot quite be connected in a satisfactory manner, I am energised enough to have a sense of closure and contentment on my final day in Sydney.

As Kurt and I pack the last items in our bags, there is a quietness around the flat. Stacey and Gavin have come to see us off, and our collective hangover creates an almost funereal atmosphere. The sadness of the group is an end-of-era sadness; there is a crushing finality to this moment, a deliberate full stop. There is something unsaid that all of us know in our hearts: that times like this will never be repeated.

And when we leave our flat for the last time and bid our sad farewells, we walk past the sign that has been written especially for me:

'To the ignorant bastard who broke this window, I'm gonna find you, and I'm gonna punch a fucking great hole right through your head. Then I'm gonna make you pay for a new window.'

relived youth

How shall we judge this reckless behaviour?

There are brazen admissions of misdemeanours ... no ... crimes - let us call them by their true name. Surely there are victims to each and every crime? And what of the wanton indulgence of all manners of narcotic and intoxicant? Is there not wisdom to be found in moderation?
What lessons are these to teach our sons and daughters?

And as these words are compellingly made for the prosecution, so too the defence must have its say.
For are there not such times in life when all stars align? When events conspire to bring such opportunity as this?
And how, when knowing how short served this may be, how conceivably can we resist this temptation?
Or indeed, should we resist?

For are there not forces at work here - hidden, subconscious even? Could this simply be an outpouring of all that has been restrained, a last gasp attempt at relived youth?
This I contend can be found even in the quietest and most carefully nurtured of childhoods. Bonds must be broken; walls must be smashed; and the spirit of youth must be unleashed on the world.

And should we feel guilty? Emphatically not.
It has been repeated, not by one, but by all involved; that this was the best of times, the happiest of times.
For this reason alone perhaps, this precious memory should be freed from debate, left unhindered, and preserved with the utmost respect that it deserves ....

4. the first journey

We reach the Mongolian border long after the sun has set. There will be a change of wheels on the train, the Chinese and Russian gauges do not match. Kurt and I opt to stay on the train to watch the process rather than wait on the platform, but it's not what we expect: the carriages are jacked up, and the wheels ingeniously slid out from underneath. The whole operation takes over an hour.

With time on our hands, Kurt and I are in contemplative mood. Our memories have been roused by that emotional encounter with Stacey in the Beijing hotel. I hugged her warmly when she came up to our room, as if everything was forgiven and forgotten, and we all sat down to talk. It turns out that she was there to take the Trans Siberian just a week after us and was travelling with a German she had met in Hong Kong. She gave us the hash that we would later smoke on the train, and an address we could stay in Berlin that belonged to her travelling companion. There was a poignant moment when she described the day after we left Sydney. She had spent the whole of it with Gavin in sombre mood. It was, of all days, the Bicentenary celebration in Australia, with a fleet of tall ships sailing in the harbour and a climactic fireworks display at sundown. Stacey described how the two of them watched all this from the roof of our apartment, both in tears. It is my last abiding memory of that time. And as we set off into the Mongolian night, I resolve firmly to put this into its rightful context, one that will consider all those paths that have led me to this place. For I am truly uncertain where I am going next ....

We awake the next day with a new routine: our Chinese carriage attendant brings us our early morning hot water which is placed on the table between our bunks; the urn will last until the afternoon, when it will be replaced. We drink our black china tea as we emerge slowly from our slumber with the blind opened only gradually at first. The beds are surprisingly comfortable - we've been supplied with fluffy down duvets and pillows to sleep on - and we have the compartment almost completely to ourselves; one of the upper bunks is empty, the other used only at night, as the occupant has friends in another carriage. It feels like first class to us.

The view now is of the Mongolian plains, a vast yellow-green expanse framed by distant hills. And with the landscape, the people are changing too. They are heavier set, and their clothing more colourful. There is something more tribal about their look than the farmers we have seen passing through the countryside of China.

We come to a halt on the second day at Ulan Bator, the Mongolian capital, and make use of a two hour stopover to take a stroll around the station. The waiting room is like a scene from a first world war movie. Sunlight casts its rays through the dusty air, and a platoon of Mongolian soldiers are strung over the benches, their dated kitbags loosely discarded around them. It appears they have been asleep for some time, mouths hung open and heads bent back at awkward angles. But for the occasional snore there is complete silence. We tiptoe through this scene without waking a soul, the room blissfully unaware of its curious foreign visitors.

As we travel on from there, the scenery changes very little, and with valium popped and head reclined, I am taken back to the beginning of my travels, where this all really started - my first solitary journey, an attempt to hitchhike across the Sahara Desert ...

It is February 1985, and I am in Tamanrasset, an Algerian desert town of no real distinction other than its strategic positioning. It is in fact the last port of call for those crossing the Sahara into West Africa. It is officially the end of the Algerian national road, although this road has been in such a state of disrepair that I have already travelled hundreds of miles alongside it in the sand.

Some of this route I have travelled by bus, and some by hitching rides on trucks. The bus was easily the worse of the two: a scrum to get tickets (for there are only two every week) and windows so dusty there is no view of outside at all. My seat had no back to it, although I am somewhat lucky to have had a seat at all; in strict order we were let onto the bus: Algerians first, then Westerners, then Africans who must sit on the floor.

And it's a bumpy ride. The sand next to the road has been compacted into corrugated ridges from the heavy traffic, causing a constant vibration through the wheels. At times I was torn between the tingling sensation of an awkwardly impending erection and a searing back pain to pull me back from the brink; to avoid embarrassment, my lap was covered strategically by a loose shirt. Although there were frequent stops to relieve these symptoms, both for Muslim prayers and for meals, it was tough going nonetheless.

The truck drive on the other hand, provided one of the best moments of my journey here. Although the cost is the same - everything has a price here - the seats in the cabin of a truck are far more comfortable, and the views of the rolling desert dunes are unhindered. After a long days drive, we stopped for the night in the middle of nowhere, a place described here in its most literal sense. From one flat horizon to another there was nothing but stars. I walked from the truck a few hundred yards to sleep in the open and take in the full canvas of the sky. For hours I laid down with exactly half the visible universe set out brightly above me, clearer than I'd ever seen before. Yet there was something else about this moment that I couldn't at first determine. What was it that made me feel so completely detached and at peace? What made the stars seem so close and so personal? And then I realised at once what it was: there was no accompanying soundtrack to this still majestic night whatsoever; just a relentless and emphatic silence ...

It has taken me four weeks of travelling to arrive at this remote outpost; after a cheap charter flight to Malaga and a ferry across the straight of Gibraltar to Morocco, I have made a long diagonal journey south through the oasis towns of Algeria. Each of these had its own magical beauty - palm fringed waters, Moorish architecture, sand dunes, salt lakes - that could still pass as the backdrop to a twenties Foreign Legion film.

But now I find myself stuck. The border south to Niger will be closed for three days due to bad weather, and there is competition for the few rides available across the desert when it finally opens. There are two ways to cross the desert: the cheaper option is a ride in the back of an Algerian truck - uncomfortable and slow, this will be my fall back position; the second option, however, is far more attractive - to pay for a ride in a car with one of the many Europeans trying to cross the desert. The town is full of Germans, French and Dutch running cars across the Sahara. Some are businessmen, taking expensive Toyota four wheel drives and minivans to sell for profit in Niger, Mali, Benin or Togo. Others are travellers like me, who plan to sell their cars to pay for their plane ticket home; they drive the cheaper cars, usually an old Peugeot 504 or Citroen 2CV.

And a lot of these drivers are stuck like me. Either their cars are broken down, their papers are not in order, or they can't get enough petrol for the crossing. Most are staying in the campsite on the edge of town, a sparse but functional plot. There is a good camaraderie, and tips are frequently exchanged and followed up: a petrol tanker is arriving tomorrow; there are eggs in the supermarket today; a driver is looking for a passenger. I spend all day asking for rides, offering information and cigarettes to new arrivals, and befriending the ones that have shown an interest. But I am not winning. I am English and male, and often I lose a promised seat to a Frenchman or a German girl at the last minute. To add to that, there is a more general problem: most drivers are wary of the extra weight a passenger will bear when struggling through the sand.

Meanwhile, food is scarce. The supermarkets have at most two or three edible items on the shelves, olives one day, sardines the next; there is no obvious pattern, just whatever the plane brought in that day. The real gold dust, though, is a freshly baked loaf of bread. There are several bakeries around town, but often they don't have flour; when they do, there's a fight to get to the front of the queue, and sometimes I am sent to the back by the police without explanation. I can spend the best part of my mornings just looking for food.

Date fruits are by far the easiest to acquire, and they are suitably nutritious. I have a shock though, when I am sharing these with a Dutchman back at the campsite. He carefully prizes open each date with his nails before eating.

"Why are you doing that?"

"To check for worms," he replies. "Didn't you know?"

"What do you mean?" I falter. I have been eating these for two weeks without a thought. He opens a few dates and then shows me one. Inside are a dozen or so thin white lines wriggling around inside.

"It's well known," he says cheerily. "About half of them have worms."

After five long days in Tamanrasset, I take a big gamble with my lift. My choice is between a truck leaving at 9 a.m., or the chance of a lift with a Frenchman at 10 a.m. I decide to hold out for the car, but then curse my luck when I find out that two Canadians have outbid me at the last minute; not only have I lost the ride, but I have missed the truck as well. In a last-ditch effort, I relate my desperate story to two Dutchmen who had been reluctant to take passengers, but had suggested they might take one in an emergency. This time, with immense relief, one of them capitulates. I am going to escape this town at last ...

For safety reasons we set off in a makeshift convoy, a motley one at that. There are two Dutch Peugeots: a saloon, in which I will travel with Johum my saviour, and an estate, driven by his friend and business partner Patrice. Joining us is a bearded Irishman on a motorbike, two Amsterdam drug dealers with matching Dobermans in a beaten up Land Rover, and a young Japanese cyclist. Astonishingly, Masa is on a solo cycling tour across Africa, although for this difficult leg of the journey his bike will be carried on the roof of the Land Rover.

There is 400 km of sand to the actual border with Niger and beyond that a further 200 km before we reach a paved road. Many deaths and disappearances are reported each year on this crossing; the main danger is straying from the route and having your tracks covered by sandstorms. There are no road markings on this stretch, apart from small black posts placed every 5 km; when the post is not there, a pile of stones usually takes its place. We have been given some good advice before setting off: always remember which side of the posts you are, and don't assume that tyre tracks are going in the right direction. If you miss a post for more than 10 km, retrace your steps.

Keeping to this loosely marked track is hard, however, when we are hit by sandstorms on the first day, and the progress is slow. When we stop to find our way, the cars often become stuck in the sand, and surprisingly it is the Land Rover that needs the most help. Its weight makes it sink further, and we extract it with traction pads wedged under the wheels and a few strong shoves. Later in the day we pass one hapless German who is having his car winched onto a truck; he has been waiting twelve days. But then we too fall foul to bad luck when the radiator suddenly bursts on our Peugeot, and we are forced to stop for the night. The sandstorm hits again as we sleep in our tents, this time far more ferociously, and in the morning we discover that the motorbike has had its paint sandblasted down to bare metal on one side. It's an oddly asymmetrical look, and a note is made to park it the opposite way round next time ...

The weather is clear on the following day, and we go a lot further. At times we drive at 70 mph to float over the sand ridges and take it easier on the suspension; it feels both reckless and exhilarating - if we hit a hole or a trench, we would surely roll the car. But Johum has asked me to look out for something at kilometre 250, and we drive much slower for this section, scanning the horizon carefully. Suddenly we spot it: a Toyota minivan lying on its side, stripped to a shell. This wreck was his own failed attempt from last year, and he poses triumphantly next to the carcass as I take his picture.

It's not the only photo shoot we have along the way. Masa has a very Japanese habit of taking his own picture every time we stop. For this he has a tripod, a camera and a video on timers. For the video he says a few words, points to his watch and then to the empty background, which to my eye has not changed at all since the last one. No doubt this will be riveting viewing for his friends back home; apart from a few boulders here and there, there are no dunes to be seen on this stretch of the desert, only a flat infinity stretching to each horizon. When we camp in the evenings, he has another technological trick up his sleeve. A slim package is removed from its carry-bag, a button pressed, and in a matter of seconds a tent springs up ready formed. We are suitably impressed, and the whole group gathers to witness this daily ritual ...

On the third day, we reach the border at In Guezzam. It is a beautiful sight, not only because we are desperate to restock our diminishing water supply, but in a very literal sense as well. For we are greeted with a spectacular view. All around this small border town the dunes are covered in Nomad tents, white and pristine, laid out in neat grid-like patterns, rising and falling with the contours; the Tuareg are in town, though strangely there are few to be seen wandering outside of their tents, and their presence is almost ghostly.

With this imposing backdrop we are processed through customs, a far quicker and easier process than it was when entering the country. I had been stuck on the Algerian border with Morocco for six days, helping three Kiwis whose Land Rover had been confiscated after customs found undeclared cash in a money belt. Algeria is particularly hard on black marketeers and force every traveller to exchange a hundred and fifty pounds in an Algerian bank. I didn't realise how much trouble they were in until we were sent before a judge. Going along as their translator, a de facto lawyer of sorts, I pleaded their case in French. The judge silenced me several times in mid sentence before talking energetically in Arabic to his consultants. After five minutes, he declared his judgement: "Trois mois, prison fermé."

Although I had managed to reduce their fine, they had just been sentenced to three months in prison. Incredibly the customs officers wanted to appeal the decision, and I was forced to leave them in limbo, fearful of being dragged into the dispute myself. I will never know what happened to them ...

And now that the customs officers have carefully checked all our bank receipts on the way out, we are able to stock up on water from the well and biscuits from the only store in town. Before nightfall we set off for Niger, until a broken exhaust stops us in our tracks only a few miles down the road, and we are resigned to spending the night in no-man's-land.

In the northern Sahara the nights had been freezing, sometimes dropping from forty degrees in the day to almost zero at night, but now the nights are warm, and I sleep without any covering in the open air. We had encountered a scorpion in our camp the previous night, and I am now cautious to check shoes and clothes in the mornings for any unwanted guests. This time though, I wake in the middle of the night to see small shapes, just visible in the moonlight, scurrying about our camp. I had felt something running over my legs, and now I can just about make them out: gerbils of some sort, quaint and harmless. Reassured, I turn over groggily and go back to sleep.

In the morning we reach the Niger border. It is marked by only a couple of huts, but there is one enterprising salesman there selling cold beers for three times their value. It is a temptation none of us can resist. Suitably refreshed, we push forward through the desert for the next town where the paved road will begin; we are nearly there.

The following day, we arrive exhausted in Arlit. It is a well resourced town; there is a bank, a campsite, restaurants and bars. And the atmosphere has changed - this is black Africa. There are street stalls and litter lining the roads, the smell of barbecued meat and the sound of African music blaring from small tinny radios. We have entered a new world.

We spend an excruciating hour registering at the police station, our thoughts preoccupied by what is to come - a properly cooked hot meal and a long cold beer. I myself haven't eaten in a restaurant for more than a month, as the cost of a meal in Algeria was prohibitively expensive. And when the moment arrives at last, I order the most extravagant item on the menu: steak and chips. But ominously, as I wait patiently sipping my beer, I am aware of something untoward developing in my stomach. By the time the dish arrives, I am altogether too sick to eat; with such deft swiftness the transformation is complete. I offer my dinner to a traveller sitting next to me, who launches into the plate with unbridled glee ...

That night, I am awoken again from my sleep, but this time there are no rodents. Instead I lie, with great discomfort, in my own shit. There has been an unheralded, and I should say unprecedented, leak in the night. When I reach the campsite toilet - a small hole at the top of a concrete mound - I squat precariously on the summit and aim as best I can. What follows is terrifying, like a scalding hot water tap bursting open from its own pressure. The pain and the sound of it are equally disturbing. It is, to use an American idiom, shock and awe.

And this will be only the first of many visits tonight, as later, lit only by a crescent moon, I negotiate the treacherous slopes of this heavily soiled volcano over and over again. I will come to remember this hole in the ground like no other I have visited before ...

It appears that everyone else is sick too. When we get to the next town, we are told that the water we took from the well at In Guezzam was contaminated with cholera. We had been boiling our water and drinking it as tea, but unfortunately we had not been boiling it for long enough. Patrice is now in hospital and may have to be flown home. My own recovery is slow - I live off rice and fanta to starve the bug - but I keep moving on, and in the next town I get another good break.

There were four Germans travelling in two Peugeots who I had met previously in Tamanrasset and bonded well with. They couldn't give me a lift back then due to the extra weight, but now they can. Without too much thought, I swap cars and bid farewell to Johum. And as simple as that, with one door closed and another one opened, a new and very different chapter of my journey begins ...

5. sub sahara

After travelling alone for so long now, reliant on the sparse services of buses and trucks, it is a luxury to find myself with good company and my own chauffeur driven car. I am in a 404 estate with Georg and Frankie, both musicians from Berlin; in the car behind us are Ecki and Adi, two close friends from Dusseldorf. Out of the window, there is a slow but joyous metamorphosis taking place. First the desert becomes scrubland, with bushes here and there; then it changes to savannah, with its green and yellow grasses surrounding small pockets of sand. We see water and agriculture appearing for the first time, and camels giving way to oxen just as Arab faces are replaced by African. And in and amongst all of this are strung the many mud-huts, that most African of structures, which remind us happily of where we are. Later on in the day, I spot a familiar sight up ahead - it's Masa, cycling at the side of the road on a racing bike laden heavily on both sides with his technological gadgets. I lean out of the car and wave to him enthusiastically; he gives a small salute in recognition and carries on pedalling.

In the towns and villages we pass through, the roads are lined with trestle tables selling food and drink. They all have a standard kit - Nescafe, condensed milk, eggs, a charcoal stove and paraffin lamps. We sit on wooden benches to have our morning coffee and omelette, and in the evenings we eat rice with stew. There is usually a period of negotiation where we try to get a fair price, but the banter is good natured; the people here are encouragingly warm and welcoming. We pick up hitchhikers as we go, on one occasion four big African women and two babies, who have to squeeze into the back seat with me. There are howls of laughter as heads and elbows are jammed into the ceiling at tortuous angles, but they are not going too far, and we drop them off safely at a nearby hospital.

Georg is a reckless driver, and this is proving to be quite entertaining. He tells me proudly how he is banned from driving in Germany, and it is clear he enjoys his own negligence. He drives slowly but with no real attention to anything else on the road. Cars and pedestrians are narrowly missed, then honked at; driving on the left side or the wrong way round a roundabout is his favourite trick. And at times he stops in the middle of the road to read a map; angry honks and diatribes from the other road users are met with a simple shrug of the shoulders.

But Georg's driving is a reflection of his own character. At 6ft 7in he has, by itself, a commanding physical presence. But his movements and reactions are so purposefully slow that it gives you the impression of a complete and unassailable confidence. At the same time his expression tells you that he doesn't have a care in the world. This combination gives him a magnetism that gains affectionate nicknames from the locals such as 'le double metre' and 'le géant'. But behind this image of a loveable rogue hides a very calculated and witty man. When his driving gets him into trouble with police, he is always able to extricate himself easily, with a bemused protestation of ignorance and a booming apology - "Oh! Oh! Oh!"

I have decided to travel with Georg to Benin now, instead of my previous plan to go through Burkina Faso to Ghana. I am reluctant to give up my ride, and I am not particularly concerned about where I end up, as long as there's a beach to be found; I've been long enough on the road now.

And Benin proves to be a fine choice. After we have left the main route through Niger, a path well trodden by the Paris-Dakar rally, there is much more of an atmosphere of innocence and discovery. The women are topless and the children naked, and large groups gather around our car peering in through the windows when we stop, like visitors to their own private zoo. When we drive past villages at Georg's slow but steady pace, we are chased for hundreds of yards with screams of "Cadeau! Cadeau! Cadeau!" by small children. The first few times this happens we stop and give out biros, but with these supplies soon exhausted we are forced to run the gauntlet. There is a lazy feel to the journey now; at one point Georg is so relaxed, leaning back and talking to me in the car, that he drives into a ditch. We wait for two hours for a passing truck to pull us out. Georg finds the whole episode quite amusing and shows no real concern for his car which is now falling apart; a piece of exhaust is left behind at the side of the road.

Soon Ecki and Adi are forced to sell their broken down car in the first Benin town that we come to, and all five of us have to squeeze into Georg's car. Nevertheless, it carries on like an old workhorse, low on its wheels and luggage bursting at the seams. At one refreshment stop in the late afternoon, we decide to quench our thirst in a roadside bar. There are three African men drinking on a nearby table who take a dislike to us as soon as we walk in. They are pompous, proud and overweight, what we will later term 'new colonialists'; for obesity here is sign of wealth. For some reason they are visibly upset by our presence, but we choose mostly to ignore them.

As we leave, Georg plonks a half drunk bottle of coke on their table and says: "Cadeau." They are incensed, and amid all the shouting one of them stands up to Georg with a lengthy diatribe. Georg puts on his confused face as I translate matter-of-factly from their African French:

"This man says he has more money than us ... you have insulted him ... he doesn't need your half drunk bottles."

"Oh, he doesn't want it then?" Georg shrugs. "Okay", and he whips the bottle away with another shrug.

We leave the bar hastily with threats of violence still ringing in our ears, the worst of it aimed at Frankie, who despite being the smallest of us is always the one who laughs the loudest ...

The road now is just a track in the terracotta earth, and as we travel further south, the vegetation becomes thicker and taller around us, until one evening we hear a cacophony of crickets. The sound marks yet another milestone as we approach the coast; but with it comes that most despised and unwelcome of creatures - the mosquito. In the night, as we sleep at the side of the road in the increasing humidity, we are woken now by their frenzied whines as they dive bomb our ears relentlessly.

And with that pest comes another, the roadblock, for we are slowly closing in on the capital. We are stopped by the police more and more frequently now, and on each occasion we are asked for a bribe of some sort. Usually this takes the form of a head peering around the inside of the car looking for a suitable gift, followed by a gruff command - "Donnez-moi ça." It is a laborious exercise, but we always hold our ground. On the second or third attempt to point something out, Georg shouts a final booming "NON!" and our passports are returned grudgingly.

In fact Georg soon decides to bypass the roadblocks altogether. Most checkpoints consist of a handful of rocks strewn across the road that can be easily navigated; now when we are waved down by police, Georg waves back with a big smile and keeps on driving. The first time he does this I am terrified, half expecting someone to shoot at us or give chase. But when we look back, we see only a shocked expression, or a comically furious blow of the whistle. It now becomes one of the most exhilarating parts of the day; the reaction is never quite the same.

And then, suddenly, we are there. We reach the sea on the fourth day and immediately find a deserted beach where we can take a swim. It feels like the finishing post to me; I have taken seven weeks to cross the Sahara from coast to coast, and this dip in the ocean feels like a celebration. In the evening there is an impromptu music session when the car is surrounded by kids. Two older boys have brought drums, and Georg plays the sax while teaching them to sing a refrain at the end of the bar with a "Ha! Ha! Ha!" With the sun low on the horizon, and a cold beer in hand, it feels like the perfect end to an epic journey for all of us.

What follows this triumphant arrival is a month of recreation, as we traverse the coast to Togo where the living is a little cheaper. There, most of the travellers are looking for a plane ticket to the next place, and the talk is awash with stories of black market deals and dodgy agents. We rent a small house with a well, and sleep outside in mosquito nets, eating at the local stalls and occasionally in the tourist restaurants. The beach is mostly deserted, and an old coastal road lies a hundred yards out to sea, lost to erosion over the last decade but creating a convenient wave break for easy swimming. In the evenings, the bars come alive with music and girls, and we indulge heavily in the locally distilled 'soda de vie' which spawns a bruising hangover.

But there is an atmosphere that begins to pervade the group over time; it changes from one of hopeful apprehension to a simmering negativity. For one by one, each of us becomes sick. First Ecki is diagnosed with malaria, then Georg is struck by something with similar symptoms, perhaps dysentery. Adi and Frankie quickly follow, though Frankie makes a recovery by drinking a local witchdoctor potion called 'yava', which apparently works by sweating out the poison. For some reason my fever comes and goes in a day. Georg says to me:

"You have the British colonial blood, you are strong. The Germans are weak."

He has plainly had enough, and within a week he buys his ticket home with the proceeds of his car sale. Frankie is the only one who wants to keep going, but he has no money; the rest - Ecki, Adi, even the Amsterdam dealers and their two Dobermans - are already booked onto flights. And after much consideration I too have come to the same unfortunate conclusion: having reached something of a dead end, I must spend the remainder of my money on a costly ticket home. It is, for me, a massive disappointment.

6. the second journey

As we approach the Russian border, I remember very clearly the despondency of that moment. Kurt and I will face a similar fate very soon. The inevitable return home is often motivated by necessity rather than desire, and the impact is that much the harder for it.

I had gone through a long period of depression following that trip. It was difficult to reconcile the richness of that experience with my drab surroundings. My friends could not relate to it with any real enthusiasm, so the stories went untold, and the sense of personal achievement in banishing demons and conquering fears was left to wilt, rather than prosper.

Nevertheless, something had changed in me. A bug had been caught; at first a quiet nagging, then an irresistible itch. I yearned for something, anything, to push me back into the fray. But it would be almost one and a half years before the next opportunity would finally present itself ...

I awake from a nightmare, upright on my knees, in a pitch black darkness. I am frozen with fear. My head is concussed, and I cannot register where I am. It is a long and tortuous moment. Slowly I recognise shapes in the room - a table here, some chairs over there, an upright piano beside me ...... and I suddenly realise: this must be where I hit my head. In my dream I had imagined a snake close by and scrambled away frantically on all fours, sleep-crawling headlong into this wooden wall. I now know where I am.

I have been sleeping the night on the conservatory floor of a large house, situated in a leafy suburb of Harare. The windows are wide open, and the rustle of the wind has stoked my vivid imagination. It is late 1986, and I have just arrived in Zimbabwe to visit my sister Bel, who has been working in one of the capital's main hospitals for the last three months. She was offered free lodgings here by a benevolent Christian family that she met through her work.

Breakfast the next morning with my new hosts is awkward, as I am obliged to explain the fresh scratches on my face through a sleep-deprived haze. But there is something else that unnerves me: it's the presence of an African servant in the room, fussing about us as we eat. I am admonished when I politely attempt to clear up my dishes. Then later, as I walk nearby along the pretty avenues fringed by purple-flowered jacaranda trees, I am approached more than once with a request for work:

"Hello sah! You need wood cutter? I good wood cutter sah!"

This is not South Africa with its abhorred Apartheid system, but it is close to how I would imagine it. I have never felt a stronger division due to the colour of my skin, and it feels shameful; it was certainly less noticeable in West Africa, where the French brand of colonialism seemed to have left behind something far more egalitarian. Nevertheless, there is no ill spirit here that I can detect - just a general acceptance of this strange imbalance of fortunes so deeply rooted in history.

And there are many throwbacks to this British colonial past that Bel and I encounter in this country. One day we are hitching back to the suburbs, when we get lucky with a lift in a beaten-up old Mercedes. The owner invites us back to his home, which sits on a small hill surrounded by rusted vintage cars and fridges. We are greeted by three barking Alsatians, and the old man leads us quickly into his dilapidated old house. With a scraggly white beard and matching white safari suit, both his character and his home are completely frozen in time. One of his hobbies is beekeeping, and he offers us home-brewed mead to drink with a friendly but sinister:

"Are you feeling anything yet?"

Throughout this display of hospitality he treats his three servant 'boys' with the same abrupt manner he treats his dogs. Bel and I, however, are made to feel like royalty, as if we are the only visitors to come this way in years. The warmth and friendliness of the white population here seems to be as strong as the black-white divide ...

In similar vein, we are invited to a tea plantation in the Inyanga national park by an Indian friend whose rich uncle is the owner. After four hours drive, we are met by a sentry guard at the end of a long winding dirt road. It is an odd apparition, as he salutes us and opens the barrier to let us through. We reach our destination several miles later as the sun goes down, the track ending on the top of a hill with a small house on its brow. The car doors are opened for us by the obligatory servant, and as we enter the house, we are greeted cordially by our host Sahti, who throws a cold beer for me to catch from behind the bar. I am suitably impressed. The place feels like a boutique hotel in the middle of a vast wilderness.

The next day reveals a magnificent view from the house, with tea bushes stretching for miles around, blanketing the rolling hills in all directions. We walk amongst them to a nearby waterfall where we are able to water-slide down rocks into a pool below. Soon we are joined by a large group of small children who watch us, captivated by this odd spectacle. Some of them carry their homemade toys with them: wire framed cars and trucks with sticks to steer them, the tyres carved from flip-flops and mounted on bottle top wheels. After giving them a few spare coins, they lead us to a nearby African village where we accept an invitation to drink beer with the tribal elders. It is called 'seven day beer' and has the appearance and smell of an alcohol induced vomit, complete with unidentifiable floating lumps; we drink with brave faces as all eyes around us watch intently. The session is finished with polite clapping, and we are on our way.

Later in the day we are taken by our host to a strange kind of country club, which is a short drive across the estate and just as isolated as the house. Welcomed by yet another saluting guard, it has the appearance of an old colonial officers mess. Inside we find ourselves the only guests amongst the billiard tables, leathered upholstery and wood panelled walls. It has a swimming pool at the back and a well-stocked bar, which we are encouraged to help ourselves to, including cigarettes. Happily ensconced, we enjoy the absurdity of the place; it has the feel of an extravagant folly, like a golf course built in the middle of the jungle for some despotic president.

The long day is rounded off with a lavish meal cooked by Sahti's wife, though changed at the last minute from fish to chicken after one of their hens was accidentally run over in the driveway. As we eat, we are told stories. Sahti is as proud as he is generous, and talks without much pause for breath about a recent visit by president Mugabe, whose helicopter landed outside his house only the week before. At this time the president is highly regarded, and Sahti can hardly contain his excitement; the moment has even been captured by a new technology hardly seen before in Africa, an expensive VHS camera.

And as we have so often encountered in Zimbabwe, we are made to feel like important guests to a stranger. We can only hope that we have given something back with our warm appreciation of this gesture and our eager ears; for that is all we have to give ...

It is of course my sister, not me, who is attracting all these favours. She is young, female and a long way from home, and her blue eyes, sun bleached hair and slight frame give her an added air of vulnerability. I accept the hospitality with good grace, despite knowing that it's unlikely I would be indulged without her. And there are a few more excursions that we wish to do before we set off on our planned journey through Malawi, Tanzania and Kenya. A car is lent to us for a week by another helpful friend, and we take a whistle-stop tour of the South, taking in Hwange game reserve - where two days of driving reveals almost every animal but a lion; Matopos national park - a mystical landscape of bald granite rocks strewn across the hills; and most impressively, the Victoria Falls. Viewed from fifty metres away, it's a stunning sight, falling over twice that distance into the gorge below, and producing its own natural rainforest and ubiquitous rainbow.

On the long drive back we pick up some African hitchhikers along the way, a young couple with a baby. They are somewhat alarmed when we stop for them, and sit silently in the back with a look of shock on their faces. We slowly become aware that, sadly, we have once again crossed one of the many unwritten codes of this divided but beautiful country.

Malawi proves to be a different type of beast. Its despotic president Banda is a renowned eccentric, who has banned long hair and beards for men, and trousers and short skirts for women. Bel will have to wear long dresses for the duration of our stay or face deportation. It has also been dictated that his photo must be hung in every establishment in the country, always higher than anything else on the wall such as paintings or clocks. However, we have heard that the country is one of the most beautiful in Africa, and after a short flight to the capital Lilongwe, we arrive suitably clothed and head for a campsite on the fringe of the town.

We have no real plans the next morning, but a fortuitous meeting at the water tap with an Australian missionary soon changes that. He is travelling the lake with an African pastor on a rare excursion away from their vocations. I ask - in hope rather than expectation - if he has room for two more in his car, and surprisingly he says yes. Ian and Pastor Chakunza each have their own stories to tell: Ian was converted to Christianity after a life-threatening motorcycle accident left him almost crippled; and the pastor was a tribal witch doctor whose extreme practices led to an epiphany. He tells us that he was the devil incarnate and had even killed as part of his craft; but it's hard for us to imagine, looking at this very timid and docile man in front of us.

There is of course an unspoken understanding that we will listen to their testimony in return for our ride, though my responses soon deteriorate into quick grunts and nods. I am least enthused when they talk about the finer details of their faith - the second baptism of Christ or some such thing - as if this complexity somehow makes their beliefs more valid; I can't really get past the first hurdle. Nevertheless, they are kind and enthusiastic travelling companions, and do not object when I commit a sin in their eyes by drinking beer. Curiously there is not only the obligatory lager available here, but also a locally brewed stout, sweet and sickly, and Chibuku, a home grown African recipe similar to the one we drunk in that village in Zimbabwe; here though, it's supplied in a milk carton, where it keeps fermenting the longer you leave it. Try as I can, I am unable to get through even one of these beers, discarding the sick smelling porridge after only a few sips ...

The journey north takes in the picturesque fishing villages and beaches of the western edge of Lake Malawi. The fishing boats are roughly hewn dugout canoes that line the shores in tidy rows, and remind you of a time long since passed. We sleep on the empty beaches at night, and bathe in the lake in the mornings. The water here is clean and clear, drinkable even.

The pastor is quiet and contemplative, but occasionally says out of the blue: "It will rain." He is usually right, and we prepare our camp accordingly. One night we watch an incredible lightning storm playing out its majestic display on the opposite side of the lake, as if for our own entertainment. It lasts for hours, the sky flashing constantly in silent rage, its sound completely lost on the wind as it slowly passes us by.

We are dropped in Karonga, a town near the northern border with Tanzania, and decide to wait there for the weekly bus to Dar es Salaam, which is some 800 miles away. It's a convenient service, saving several bus changes, and is due in three days time. But soon after we arrive, we hear of some worrying problems at the border: many travellers have been sent back due to incomplete documents; most commonly their vaccination book is missing a yellow fever jab. At the mention of this, Bel's face drops. Despite having worked in an African hospital, it appears she doesn't have one.

And so begins an escalating crisis. The solution is not immediately forthcoming: there is nowhere in town to get the jab, and if there were, we are not prepared to wait the ten days it would take to become valid. For a while we are resigned to taking our chances, but on the day before the bus is due we encounter a Dutchman who offers a solution. As a seasoned traveller, he has in the back of his Land Rover a range of counterfeit stamps we can use for the vaccination certificate. He is leaving town soon, however, and we drive hastily back to the hotel to stamp the book. Instead, after five minutes of nervous waiting, Bel emerges from the room in tears; she cannot find her vaccination book. In fact she cannot even find her passport ...

The next morning at 6 a.m. the weekly bus arrives, and I search intently through the dusty windows for a sighting of my sister ... it's a huge relief when I spot her amongst the passengers. A moment later, her passport is flashed at me with a smile. She has managed to retrieve it from Mzuzu, a town about a hundred miles back where she was almost certain she'd left it in the bank. I had remained in Karonga at the police station trying to locate it over the phone, while she had hitchhiked back to Mzuzu alone. I was unsure if she would have found it, let alone have caught the bus.

After a few hours drive down a dusty track, we reach the border controls at Songwe. An orderly queue forms outside the immigration hut, and I stand in front to get my documents checked first. With my passport duly stamped, Bel arrives at the desk.

"You don't have yellow fever. Go back to Malawi and get your jab," says the border guard.

"Please, I work in a hospital. I've had the jab, I just lost the paper."

"Go back to Karonga," he intones. Immediately an apology is proffered, tears are shed, and my passport stamp to Tanzania waved at him in mitigation - we can't possibly be separated.

"Go back to Karonga," he repeats. At this, Bel holds out a banknote worth a few dollars, our last resort ...

"What is that? Is that a bribe?" The man, clearly insulted, waves her to one side. "Wait here!"

We stand aside as the last passengers are processed, until finally we are the only ones left in the room.

"How dare you offer me a bribe in front of all these people!" His eyes quickly turn to some documents on his desk which he starts to busy himself with. We are unsure how to respond, and a silence permeates.

"Ten dollars," he mutters under his breath.

Bel duly empties her wallet, which reveals about five dollars worth of local currency. With great reluctance he takes what she has and stamps her passport. Back on the bus, we embrace in a moment of elation and relief; it's the end of our ordeal, and we've somehow emerged unscathed. But surprisingly, it is not the last we would see of that border guard ...

The bus travels slowly, unbelievably slowly. We could probably stretch our legs walking alongside with no risk of it getting away from us. Going uphill it is slowed by the incline, and going downhill it is slowed by the gears because the brakes are completely shot. At one stage we crash through a police barrier, inconveniently located at the bottom of a steep incline, and travel fifty metres down the road before stopping. There are numerous breakdowns to interrupt our journey - overheating, stalling, flat tyres; and an ongoing battle inside the bus to open the windows - we need to cool down from the tropical heat, but the locals don't like the draft.

The first stop for the night on this three day journey is at Kyela. We go out in search of dinner but there is nothing there; no electricity, no food, no drink, no toilets. And when we return to the bus to sleep, our bag of provisions, containing all our food and cigarettes for the trip, has been stolen. There is a night watchman and several passengers who all tell us that they saw two women enter the bus, rustle around at the back and leave with our bounty. It is hard for us to understand why no one has even tried to intervene. That night we go to sleep hungry and resentful.

The following day, however, we have a change of luck, as breakfast is conjured up from thin air. Bel runs into the very same border guard that we bribed the day before, who it transpires is travelling on the same bus as us; he is sympathetic to our plight and buys us both a generous meal at a roadside cafe. Moreover, he soon becomes a good friend and supplies us with cigarettes for the rest of the trip. By the time we reach our destination two days later, we calculate he has repaid us every penny of the bribe.

Dar es Salaam proves to be a crumbling city, with its roads, buildings and ships lying idly in disrepair. There is not much to see that we're aware of, so we stop only briefly on our way to the Kenyan coast. The change across the border is like a breath of fresh air; we are greeted by a tarmacked road fringed with palms and flowering shrubs; then, as if in acknowledgement, the sun obligingly peeps out of the clouds. It's been a gruelling bus ride through Tanzania, and our minds are now firmly set on the white sands of Malindi. However, before we can progress, one urgent stopover is required at the Mombasa general hospital ...

I have been recently visited by a plague of boils. It started in Harare where the first one appeared, innocently at first, on the left side of my buttocks. Over the course of a week it grew to disproportionate size and had to be lanced, so I went to the hospital where my sister worked. A medical student volunteered to do the job, grasping the scalpel with a hesitance that did little to quell my anxiety. As various nurses and hospital staff walked in and out of the room with my pale white cheeks ceremoniously on display, he made one tentative jab after the other, but with no success. Finally, with the scalpel raised high enough for a good swing, the blade pierced through the scab and sunk deep into the wound. I was literally stabbed in the arse.

This time though, I have a boil on my thigh. It is bigger than the previous, almost an inch across, and the pain has made it difficult to walk. I queue for half an hour at the casualty desk, where a very tired looking doctor writes me a note on a small piece of paper. Next to me, a man is dripping blood on the floor from a hand mangled by machinery and wrapped in a blood soaked shirt. I have been directed to another part of the wing, which I find easily by following his trail of blood through the hospital corridors. After two hours sitting on the floor with my fellow sufferers, I am approached by a three foot six hunchbacked nurse. She beckons me with her finger in a suitably menacing fashion, like Ygor from a Frankenstein movie:

"Come this way ..."

She shuffles along, leading me further up the same red-spotted trail to a small surgery. The room is bare except for an operating table, and both the floor and the table are stained heavily with dried blood. Nevertheless, I am desperate to have the boil lanced. The surgeon asks me if I would like an anaesthetic and, relieved to see the syringe immersed in disinfectant, I gratefully accept the offer. Without the pain to endure this time, I watch with wonder as the muscle and bone of my leg is revealed to me in the greatest detail.

There will be more abscesses like this to visit me when I return to England, always forming coincidentally on the left side of my body, but with no diagnosis forthcoming. The best informed guess that my GP will come to offer me is:

"So .. er .. how is your hygiene? Do you shower very often?"

And now, with pestilent boils purged, we travel onwards to Malindi. This coastal town is an old port which now caters to all manner of tourists; locals, travellers and package tours alike. There are long sandy beaches and boat trips to the reef for snorkelling. We quickly discover that we can swim in the pools of the four star hotels by buying lunch and drinks there, while sleeping in a cheap African hotel in the town centre. Halfway through our stay, our room cleaner offers to wash our clothes for a small fee. On our day of leaving, there is a letter from him lying on the bed:

By room-steward, PO Box 123, Malindi.

> *My dear madarm and sir,*
> *The above words concerns my full home address. Telling you the truth, I'm please with what you did to me the day before yesterday. I say thank you very much.*
> *But my problem is: I don't have a watch for keeping my work regularly. Would you please help me with one watch if you have any!*
> *Could you please write me your full address before you leave so that I can write to you for friendship and rememberance, I now find you my best friends and helpers.*
> *How happy and thankful would be if:*
> *1) You help me with your address,*
> *2) We become friends,*
> *3) I get the requested wrist-watch.*
> *Yours obediently,*
> *EVANS*

Evans has of course spotted that I wear a rather nice digital watch. We leave him our address, but not unfortunately the watch; I am confident that he has procured all kinds of gifts from previous guests with this charming method. A second letter with the same request awaits us nevertheless on our return home ...

Next, we take the scenic route to Nairobi - a slow train from Mombasa, where we can sleep overnight in a bunk - and book a camping safari as soon as we arrive. It's the culmination of our trip and a big expense, and fortunately the experience does not disappoint. We camp openly in the

Masai Mara, with our tents guarded at night by a Masai warrior, and an ex-British-army cook conjures up exquisite meals cooked on an open fire. Crucially, we see lions and cheetahs, but now so many that we become almost immune to their charms; it doesn't help that the spell is often broken by a stream of circling minibuses every time we spot a pride.

Back in Nairobi I find myself with a few spare days to wait for my flight back home. Bel has left already, and I have been challenged by an acquaintance to stay all night long at the Modern Green Bar in Latema Road. It is one of the more infamous bars of Nairobi and is never known to have closed its doors. The beers are bought through a small opening in a wire cage, and most of the clientele are already drunk when we arrive. We are generously bought beers by two locals, who periodically threaten to fight each other, then quickly make up. The conversation repeatedly goes like this:

"Are you American?"

"Actually we're English."

"American! Good! We love America! My name is Ali, this is my cousin."

Later we are surrounded by four bar girls who demand we buy them drinks. I buy a beer for one of them in the vain hope of making peace, but this only creates further disharmony amongst the group. As a reaction to my apparent coolness towards her, the girl says to me:

"I like you, but you are too proud."

"I'm not proud," I protest.

"So why don't you like me? You don't like black girls?"

But once they realise we're not going to sleep with them, they soon leave us alone. It's a long night, and there are many fights that we have to steer clear of. But then finally, at 6.a.m., we witness the moment we have been waiting for. The barman comes out from behind his cage with his broomstick and quietly starts sweeping the floor, now thick with bottle tops and cigarette ends. And there it is; I have done what I set out to do. I have seen it.

As the local saying goes:

'Have you seen .. the Green Bar clean?'

7. the third journey

As we cross the border into Russia, there is only a perfunctory search of our bags by the officials. There are many people on the train taking Chinese goods to sell in Russia and, like us, little scrutiny is given to these capitalist traders. This is the time of Gorbachev, and the cold war is now in its deepest thaw.

A restaurant car is attached to the train, but we have no roubles to buy food yet, and stick to our chilli meat crackers washed down with tea. Now passing us by is Lake Baikal, the most voluminous lake in the world, and for long periods of time the train hugs the southern shoreline, the waves almost lapping the wheels. The costumes of the people change once again, back to greys this time, but the transition is slower in their faces; for hundreds of miles the features are still clearly Mongolian. When these in turn become more European, so too does their stature, now heavy boned and broad, as if to cope with the harsher winters. We are heading north.

As these gently progressing landscapes pass us by, Kurt and I talk about how we met, and how that moment shaped a year in both of our lives. Barely five months after my return from East Africa, I had packed my bag once again, this time headed for Thailand. With no need for camping equipment, I carried a small sports bag - lighter, less conspicuous, more liberating - with only a few change of clothes and a cut-down guidebook. I had been told that the travelling would be easier than in Africa, and it proved to be significantly so. Instead of the hard bus rides, there are air-conditioned coaches with video, running on smoothly paved roads; instead of the blandly cooked food, there are stir fried noodles and coconut milk curries, even a Western menu if you so desire. Cheap beach huts line the empty beaches of the South, and cafes boast the latest bootlegged Hollywood videos to attract their clientele. And the Thai people are genuinely charming. They are friendly, welcoming and meticulously polite. Most are Buddhists, a faith that seems to permeate an inner peace in its practitioners here. Nevertheless, beneath the surface is a steely self respect; this is a country that is proud to have never been colonised.

Kurt had arrived in Bangkok after a year travelling in Indonesia and Australia with his sister, and was on his way up north. I had just spent five weeks travelling around Thailand with an ex-girlfriend, something that had proved to be a predictable mistake, and had just booked a flight to Hong Kong, heading for China on my own. But over the next few days, as Kurt and I drank long into the night, there was a friendship born that was hard to ignore. More than anything, I sensed an opportunity to travel with someone like-minded for once. And so, the day before the flight, I cancelled my ticket ...

It's April 1987, and Kurt and I have just finished a hill trek north of Chiang Mai. We are travelling with Kenny, a Chinese Malaysian, and his girlfriend Evelyn from Austria, who we met in Bangkok on one of those late night whisky sessions. The trek had been one of the less touristic ones, to an area near the Burmese border where Westerners rarely visit, and although both fascinating and rewarding as a result, it was memorable for more dispiriting reasons. On the first day Evelyn had fallen out with a girl on our expedition, a twenty-something Fijian called Julie, who had carelessly thrown litter into the jungle. After castigating her publicly, the following few days saw a divide open up between two different factions of our ten-strong group, and the atmosphere grew heavier each day. The girl complained constantly to our Thai guide: the huts were dirty, the food was plain, the trek was boring, there was too much opium smoking; she clearly didn't belong. It was something of a relief then, to return to Chiang Mai afterwards.

But now, only a few days later, there is a sting in the tail. Awaking to screams and shouts, we discover that a package has been delivered to our hotel. Though addressed to Evelyn, it has been opened by the Thai wife of the British owner, who suspected something was wrong and opened it regardless. The package contains a generous specimen of human shit, and comes with a note: 'Regards, from Julie'. The hotel owner, a tattooed ex-army sergeant, is incensed:

"I'm going to get that bitch," he tells us. "I've sent my boys to every bus and train station in Chiang Mai. I've told them to plant heroin on her and call the police. She's going to spend the rest of her life in jail. "

We are not convinced that the punishment fits the crime, but apparently his wife's honour is at stake, and no amount of persuasion from us will change his mind. In the evening he reports back to us: every station was checked, but she apparently got away. She will never know how close she came to a lifelong stay in the 'Bangkok Hilton' ...

Leaving this behind, the four of us decide to head north towards the Golden Triangle, the junction where Burma, Laos and Thailand meet. On the first day, two long bus rides take us to Thaton, a quaint little village where a hilltop Buddhist temple looks out over the Mekok River. After considering taking a three hour motor boat ride downstream to our next stop Chiang Rai, we discover there is an altogether more interesting option: for 40 U.S. dollars we can have a raft built, and float down the rapids instead. The trip will take three days.

We watch the next day as the raft is constructed piece by piece by the local craftsmen, using bamboo floated down the river from a source upstream. At first a base appears, then a low wall, then a thatched roof for the middle section, and lastly a built-in helm at the back. After several hours work it has become a thing of beauty, our very own bamboo house boat. The design is practical too: at fifteen feet by four, it's just big enough for the four of us to sleep on, and the roof will provide shelter from sun and rain.

The first days rafting is easy; there is a gentle current, and we keep cool by floating in the river next to the raft, carried down peacefully by it's muddy brown waters. Sometimes there are minor rapids to negotiate, which we manage with one at the helm and two poles front and back to push off the rocks, but most of the day passes serenely by. As the light starts to fade, we pull up under a tree next to a Lahu village. Kurt and I venture into the village looking for food and ganja, but the village is pitch black now, and we are surrounded by barking dogs. After one futile attempt at conversation with an old woman, we retreat to the raft, resigned to an early night. But just as we are about to lay down, the sound of muffled voices rises from the nearby trees. Suddenly there are ten torches moving down the bank towards us. None of us speak, but we are all thinking exactly the same thing: we've heard of armed robberies in this area recently, including a fatal shooting, and here we are by the side of the river, four sitting ducks.

But amongst the bouncing beams of light, there is a strange object that I can make out, a silhouette of something familiar ...

"It's a bong!" I shout triumphantly.

Minutes later, with five of the Lahu tribe weighing down heavily on one end of our raft, the other five watching from the bank, we smoke from a two foot bamboo bong with these happy strangers. There is very little communication, except for one anxious moment when I am introducing myself and one of them grabs a knife; later we realise that my name must translate into 'knife' in Lahu.

After our visitors have left us for the night, the release of tension and the effects of smoking the grass soon have us in stitches. To encapsulate the moment, Kenny benefits us with some of his cultural humour:

"Old Chinese saying: never park your raft under a tree."

On the second day, we are challenged by much heavier white water rapids. Kurt is the de facto captain of the ship, barking out orders from the helm as Kenny and I push off the rocks with bamboo poles. At one point we damage the raft, forced sideways by the current against a large rock. However, when we emerge largely unscathed from the fastest one of all, we are reminded of our luck when we see the broken remains of an old house raft lying on one of the banks. There is a school and shop on the opposite bank, and we stop to have lunch and stock up on provisions. Before we set off, I offer sweets to a small group of uniformed children. One by one, without a teacher to prompt them, they walk up to me, take a graceful bow, and receive their sweet like a book from a prize-giving. It's a magical moment.

As we continue down the river, we ready ourselves for a mid-afternoon encounter. By now, we have grown accustomed to the motor boat passing us once a day in each direction, with several tourist cameras poised to snap our house raft as they draw close. Today we have made a sign that reads 'No photos please', and as the afternoon boat goes past, we hold up the sign and shout out the words in unison. There is a wonderful puzzled look that appears across their faces; all cameras are frozen, and the picture passes them by.

Another succession of rapids on the third day, and the raft is leaning precariously to one side. It is still functional, however, and we make a lunch stop at another village on the bank. As we go looking for food, Kurt and I come across a game of foot volley being played, where a basket-woven ball must be kept in the air with a maximum of three touches on each side of a tennis-like net. We join in the game, one on each side, and my team wins 11-6. There's a warm camaraderie generated from this casual encounter, almost as if the game has been prearranged. Hand shakes are exchanged energetically, and we are on our way.

Further on, we find ourselves in a narrow alleyway leading to the village. A rogue elephant appears at the other end, striding towards us, its flanks scraping the fence on each side. It's not going to stop. Kurt looks at me with a smile and starts humming the James Bond theme tune. We both dive theatrically through the wooden railings into someone's back yard. Dishevelled but unharmed, we are rewarded by a noodle stall around the corner.

The run-in to Chiang Rai on the fourth day is slow and stuttering. The river has now widened and is so shallow in parts that we are often stuck on sandbanks. It becomes hard work to keep the raft moving through the current, so there is a collective feeling of relief when we are finally able to moor on the town jetty. A man, conveniently waiting at the wharfside, negotiates the purchase of our house for the princely sum of three dollars, enough for us to buy a couple of beers. The state of our raft, with roof now leaning at 45 degrees, is of no consequence; the bamboo will be salvaged and reused.

Once settled in Chiang Rai, we hire motorcycles and ride up to the Burmese border, and then on to the Golden Triangle. It is a beautiful part of the country, and with bikes we are able to explore away from the main roads, cutting through the tribal villages and paddy fields along the way. But as we approach the end of our trip to the North, and bid farewell to

Kenny and Evelyn, my thoughts turn back to the tricky subject of where I am going next ...

It is a common pitfall of travelling that you find yourself holed up in cities for much longer than you would normally desire. The city is not only a transit hub to get you to the next place, it is also the place to get your visa, your plane ticket or your money wired. Sometimes it is just a place you end up because there is no particular direction you are heading. And so it was for Kurt and I, when we returned to Bangkok from our trip up north.

We stay at the PB guest house in Khaosan Rd, one of the oldest buildings in the street, complete with grand wooden staircase and resident monkey patrolling the balustrades; upstairs are the rooms, and downstairs is the snooker hall where you can buy bags of ganja from the old lady at the door. And we have invented our own game - 'bed tennis' - to while away the time, stoned in our room. Each has his own makeshift bat - mine is a water flask, his an address book - and we knock a ping pong ball to each other between the two beds for as long as possible. Today the official world record for a rally reached eighty-nine. Occasionally we collapse in hysterics just as we approach a new one.

For we are comfortable in each others presence now. There is something laid bare in a friendship of this kind between two different nationalities in a far off place. There is no context of social divisions from our different countries to concern ourselves with, no prejudgment, conscious or otherwise, of accents or towns where we grew up, or where we went to school. Most of these barriers do not exist. And Kurt has grown up on a diet of British humour; with the BBC broadcasting as far as Amsterdam, he's followed all the alternative comedy shows such as 'Monty Python' and 'The Young Ones'. This makes it easy for us to do something we both like doing immensely; indulging in absurd and humorous lateral thinking. Or in other words, just talking shit ...

In the evenings we mix with the other travellers in the street and swap stories. Before the invention of the internet, this is one of the best places to get information from all over the world. Mekong whisky and coke is the staple diet here, as beer is beyond the traveller's budget, and the combination of whisky and caffeine has a similar effect to speed. It is in this inspirational environment that we have formulated a plan. The next weeks and months are laid out clearly in front of us. We will, with military precision, execute the following duties as noted in my diary:

1) Apply for our work visas for Australia at the embassy here, dressed in appropriately neat and tidy attire.
2) Proceed by bus to Penang, Malaysia to purchase a cheap plane ticket.
3) Take the next available flight to Sydney.
4) Work and travel around Australia - to be determined how much.
5) Return to Thailand for some R+R.
6) Fly to Hong Kong, then by train to Beijing to get the Trans Siberian home.

As it turned out, there was to be only one major detour from this plan. We were yet to know this, but the flight to Hong Kong would come with a free stopover. And so it was divined that in March 1988, after our return to Thailand from Sydney, we would spend two unscheduled months in the beautiful archipelago islands of the South China Sea known as the Philippines ...

8. the island

We have the shore in sight now. It's taken ten days of island hopping to get to this point. Starting out from the mean streets of Manila, where each shop or business has a security guard armed with everything from a second world war Luger to a modern day Kalashnikov, we have traversed southern Luzon, Mindoro, Tablas and Romblon to get here. There have been scenic rides through paddy fields and lush tropical plantations, squeezed shoulder to shoulder on the back benches of rainbow coloured Jeepneys, a form of shared taxi. And nights spent in bamboo cabins built over the water on stilts, sipping the ubiquitously cheap San Miguel beer. There have been boat rides on modern catamarans escorted by dolphins, and on smaller motor boats crammed with itinerant traders and their assortments of local produce. The water is turquoise and transparent in the harbours, and the beaches are white and empty.

I have also spotted a shark along the way; a fin, almost three feet tall, rose out of the sea alongside us and cruised for a few minutes, matching us for speed before sinking gracefully back down again. It must have been the length of our boat. The Philippines have regular sinkings, the ferries often overloaded and unstable, and there are rarely any survivors in these shark infested waters. And now our boat, which is en route to Panay, slows down to drop us at our requested stop. As we wade to shore with trousers rolled up, our feet touch for the first time the warm soft sands of our destination.

Borocay is a small and narrow island only three miles long, but already has a reputation amongst travellers. It will eventually become a big tourist destination, but right now there is no electricity and only a limited amount of construction, mainly of bamboo. We find a place to stay in the middle of the village run by a German, Heiner, and his Filipino wife. Over the following weeks we will come to know Heiner very well. He spent six years travelling, mostly in India, before buying a piece of land on Borocay and building this guest house with his own hands. He is particularly proud of having the only pool table on the island. This table has made a similar journey to ours, by Jeepney and boat from Mindoro, and needing six men

63

to carry it ashore. He has game rules in place to help pay back his investment: winner-stays-on, with the challenger paying one cent per game. We estimate it will take him ten years to recoup the costs. His laissez-faire attitude to money is also apparent in his scrutiny of the paying guests. We are carefully vetted when we first arrive before he will admit to having any rooms available. Then, later in our tenure, one of the other room occupants is evicted after only one night's stay. I ask him why:

"He was singing in the shower," he says, matter-of-factly.

"That's all? What's so bad about that?"

"They were fucking Christian songs!" he explains.

The days on Borocay are lazy, there can be no other way to describe it. We are woken briefly by the predawn fanfare of cockerels, then drift slowly back to sleep; this intrusive noise is everywhere in the Philippines, cock fighting is a national pastime. When we get up, our breakfast is already on the veranda, hanging from the roof to escape the attention of the ants: fresh rolls delivered by the island baker. Soon after, a family of pigs walk past, noses to ground, as they venture on their daily forage around the island; and occasionally a buffalo strolls by purposefully, on it's way to some unknown destination.

A mid morning joint is then requisite to set the tone, followed by a walk down the beach and a swim. Book reading, or several games of backgammon will likely round off the morning; I am reading Graham Greene's 'The End of The Affair', a book that has some resonance after my tryst with Stacey.

Lunch is taken at one of the beach side cafes, perhaps the pseudo Mexican restaurant, in which every dish on the menu is just a rearrangement of minced beef, beans and salad with the odd taco thrown in; we have, however, found a way of spicing it up with some newly discovered sweet chilli sauce. After that, more of the same, and an afternoon nap may or may not take place depending on the heat. Then as the light draws in, my favourite part of the day is upon us ...

When the sun sets here, it is spectacular. I prime myself with a smoke just beforehand, then lie on my back in the warm shallow waters waiting for the show to begin. What follows is like a living, breathing Renaissance painting, with shapes and colours slowly transforming before my eyes. The clouds are perfectly carved cumulonimbus, theatrically backlit with yellows, then oranges, then the deepest reds. When one drifts off, another more majestic cloud takes its place. All this is reflected perfectly in the gentle waters that shimmer around my feet like liquid mercury. By the time the show is over, I have been floating there for almost an hour.

As night draws in, the oil lamps around the island are lit, and the small huddles of lights that scatter the beach front impart a conspiratorial air. In our particular huddle we play long sessions of pool while keeping tabs on our growing consumption of San Miguel. Travel stories are exchanged with Heiner and his Kiwi business partner Angus, who he met while travelling in India. Angus is a six foot tall redhead with fully grown beard, who regales us with stories from Afghanistan where his countenance in their culture meant he was treated like a god. Heiner is a good but bitter man; although a hippy at heart, he presents a hard shell to the world. When he was young, he spent six months in a German prison for possession of cannabis, a minor offence in most countries. He is philosophical about this strangely skewed outlook of the justice system and has these wise words to give to the world's governments:

"Every politician should be made to take acid. It should be in every constitution. It's the only way for them to see the truth."

We smoke and play doubles into the night. It feels like these two are some kind of future vision of Kurt and I, who after years of wandering have found a home on some deserted island. The only thing that's missing for us is the money.

That night I have a dream. I am looking out of a plane window, coming in to land at Heathrow airport. It is cold, grey and overcast outside the tiny porthole, and I am filled with the anxiety of having no money and no job to return to. I awake with a start, and the room comes slowly into focus. The first thing I see is a palm tree through an opening in the thatched roof. Then a cockerel sings.

And I am happy with the world.

the life of a traveller

What can we say about the life of a traveller?

First let me declare what many a hard working citizen will scream out loud: Behold the lazy and the irresponsible, the user and the taker!

For who that lives in a rich country and travels in poor is not an exploiter of sorts? Do they not carry the echoes of those shameful days of slavery and colonialism that our very own ancestors found so easy to indulge?

And even if these discretions can be reasoned or excused, there are others who will ask: where is the achievement or purpose in any of these exploits, beyond the simple lure of a cheap excursion?

To the accusations of irresponsibility, the plead must be guilty as charged. For the young are, by definition, without the responsibility that will burden them later in life; yet neither do they carry the physical burden of old age, one that will quickly render this nomadic life a discomfort too hard to bear.

And as to financial exploitation: guilty with mitigation. For the forces that create the inequalities and injustices of this world are beyond the traveller's grasp. The world is as they find it. And this world belongs to those guilty souls with the power and the riches to change it.

But for the third more serious charge of futility, an emphatic cry of not guilty resounds. For as the memoirs of this particular traveller bear witness, the lessons learnt are the lessons of life, and the frequency and strength of these are that much more when beyond the comforts of ones sheltered home.

And from this testimony I would also ask this:
Where are the well worn cliches? Where are the claims of finding oneself or crossing landmarks off a list?

There are none. Only the characters encountered, the friendships made and the experiences shared are left as indelible prints, as are the moments of exhilaration when adversity meets good fortune.

It is a life in macrocosm, a wilful exposure to all of life's diversity, its richness and its beauty, its turmoil and its madness. And one that only the lucky few can choose to live ...

9. freedom

Now, as the train heads west across the Siberian plains, we look for an opportunity to exchange our wares for roubles at every station along the way. It's not until we pull into Novosibirsk with a two hour scheduled stop that we get our chance: two young men in western dress, a telltale sign, are scouting the platform looking for trade. They are brash and confident when we approach them, and we are down to business with very little ceremony. Surprisingly, they are keen on the unfashionable jeans that Kurt has bought, although their taste in music is a little more subversive; the tape that gets the highest price is the Sex Pistols. We ask for vodka, and they return later with two bottles bought to order. A good days business is had by all; but importantly for us, we are now flush with roubles and can finally eat a cooked meal in the restaurant car.

As evening falls and we enter the carriage, there is a strangely subdued atmosphere that greets us; the place is almost full, but only a few quiet murmurings can be heard amongst the clinks of knives and forks on plates. Soon we understand why: a large woman appears in front of us, blocking our way, with such formidable demeanour that she can best be described as a battle-axe. She points fiercely at an empty table and barks out two Russian commands, easily interpreted as 'Sit down there! Hurry up!'. A menu is slammed onto the table in front of us, and she marches off purposefully. It is clear who is the master of this realm. For a while there are suppressed giggles and smirks around the room, like a classroom still shocked by the strictness of a stand-in teacher.

When she returns, she is suddenly taken by my hair. A barely perceptible smile breaks out from her stoic features as she grabs my head with two hands and runs fingers through my spikes.

"Aaah! Lipky!" she says knowingly, which after a moments thought I take to mean hair gel. We have formed an awkward bond: she too has short cropped hair, perhaps hair gel is hard to come by in Russia. And from that encounter a routine has been born; from now until Moscow, there will always be a welcoming hand to rub my hair whenever I sit down to eat. The food, when it arrives, is unexceptional, but it is the thrice daily performance of our host that we will most look forward to for the remainder of our journey.

Through the window now we are beginning to see a more industrial landscape, and with it the brutalist architecture that I have come to imagine all of Russia to be; concrete, grey and oppressive. The image of a repressed people that this conjures up is in strong contrast to how I feel at this moment, looking out from my comfortable cocoon. These last few years I have been experiencing a freedom that is almost unthinkable to the vast population outside. And I am truly appreciative. For it has not always been so ...

It's early 1981, and I am busking in Cirencester, next to a statue in a small picturesque square. The sun is out, as is our hat, and I am strumming the guitar in a duet with my partner Ben. We are singing Rolling Stones numbers mostly - 'Walking the Dog', 'Have Mercy', 'Dead Flowers' - but we have also composed a few of our own, in similar RnB style. One of them is called 'My advice':

Standin' on the corner, woman comes up to me (she said)
I can solve your problem, my advice ain't fuckin' free
But that's alright (right my baby), that's alright (right my baby)
that's all right (right right right), that's all right (right right right)
She said I'll solve your fuckin' problem but ...
My advice ain't fuckin' free.

And one that's a bit less offensive, 'Praise the lord' in gospel style:

I've seen thunder, I've seen rain
I've seen women, livin' in low down sin
See my old man, never does a stroke of work
See my old lady, she's goin' berserk (so I say)
Hallelujah praise the lord, Hal-le-lu-jah pra-ise the lord ...
I went down to the local missionary, a man came up to me
He said: now come on son, all you gotta do today

Is get down on your knees and pray, oh lord (and I say)
Hallelujah praise the lord, Hal-le-lu-jah pra-ise the lord ...

There's a drunk here now, balancing precariously on his haunches as he tries to throw a coin into the hat from about ten feet away. After several misses, we are eagerly eyeing up the small fortune amassing on the pavement; this could be our most lucrative session in days. But when he finally gets one in, our hopes are dashed; instead of leaving the near misses, he picks up the coins one by one and staggers on down the road. A change of luck awaits us at a nearby takeaway, however; as we carefully count our coins out to pay for two burgers, a woman takes pity and leaves a banknote on the counter.

Ben and I, both eighteen, are enjoying our first year of freedom after finishing school the previous summer. We had been in a band together there, he on guitar and I on drums, and this spring's escapade of busking around England came together spontaneously when we both found time on our hands. We are sleeping on the floors and sofas of friends and family, and the busking income is our beer money. Drinking in pubs and playing pool is a favourite hobby of ours now that we have been set free from the shackles of parents and teachers alike. And the dedication with which we indulge this habit could easily give the impression of making up for lost time.

For we are both products of a school system designed to create the accountants and engineers of this world. A machine that seeks to take its diverse raw ingredients and shape them into one homogenous but marketable commodity at the end of the line. And it is a mould we will never fit. For we are the unwilling participants of that antiquated social engineering enterprise known as boarding school. Although an obscure one, without the pomp and ritual of the more historic public schools, it nevertheless had the semblance of being in the army, locked away as we were in barracks with a group of puerile adolescents. And it had, unfortunately, the opposite of its intended effects; I came away with a distaste for all those conventional middle class aspirations that were so tacitly assumed.

But there is a twist. For although I am a misfit, certainly of attitude and aspiration, I am far from being a reject. I have in fact secured a place at Oxford university, for I have an ability that comes easily to me without too much application: I can do maths. And the irony is not lost on me. The fact that I will soon move to another outdated institution is tempered by my knowledge of two things; firstly, my accommodation and fees will be met comfortably by a council grant; secondly, I will have enough free time to indulge in other pursuits while I'm there. My overriding passion is music - even now, as Ben and I sing for our beer, plans are in place for a three piece band based in Oxford.

And there is a fresh confidence about me now, something that's come hand in hand with my new found freedom. I have recently returned from working in Switzerland, where a basic wage is double that of the UK, and have bought a car with the proceeds. It was my first ever job, and an experience that would set the pattern for many years to come ...

I arrive by train in the centre of Geneva in the summer of 1980. It's a pretty lakeside town, straddling the River Rhone as it leaves the southern shore of Lac Leman. In the middle of the bay is its famous landmark, a water jet that surges four hundred feet into the sky. It is satirically known as the 'drinking fountain' by neighbouring cantons in reference to Geneva's big-mouthed inhabitants, but I am largely immune to this observation; for my understanding of spoken French is poor.

I take in this magnificent view while waiting nervously outside the Manpower temp agency, an office that sits with pride of place on the Quai des Bergues. After rehearsing my lines a few times, I finally take the plunge and walk inside.

"Je cherche du travail. N'importe quoi," I say as casually as possible.

"J'ai une passporte Suisse," I explain further, flashing my shock-red proof of citizenship in front of them; I'm fortunate enough to have dual nationality, having acquired Swiss through my late grandfather. My poor French lends me an air of innocence and vulnerability, and the women at the desk compensate by being overly helpful and polite: they help me to fill in forms and let me use their office as a home address. Later, after a long search on foot armed with a tourist map, I find a cheap room to stay at some university lodgings that have been emptied of students for the holidays; clean and functional, the room has a bed and a desk, with communal kitchen and bathroom down the corridor. And with those basic formalities complete, all that remains now is to wait patiently for that offer of employment ...

Every day that follows is filled with morning and afternoon trips to the agency to check on my status, each met with a breezy "Pas encore, monsieur." The rest of the time I spend in parks, eking out my meagre funds by eating cheap supermarket food. But after several days without word of a job, I have almost nothing left. On a Friday night, with just enough money for one night's board in my pocket, I decide to blow it all on beer in a bar near the centre of town.

It is a final fling of defeat. If ever there was a case of drowning sorrows in a beer glass, then this is surely it. I am facing failure at the first attempt - money will have to be sent out, sleeping in doorways considered, and a return home likely with tail held firmly between legs. My face is a perfect picture of despair.

But as the night progresses, a group on the next table invite me to drink with them. It's not long before my story is coaxed out of me piece by piece, and immediately I am pulled back from the brink; Jeanot and Gabrielle, a couple in their thirties, offer me a place to stay while I get back on my feet. They drive me back to the student lodgings to retrieve my bag, and then to their home, a short drive out of town. Jeanot tells me with immense pride that it will be no problem for me to stay, only last week they had managed to put up an entire brass band.

Jeanot turns out to be a crossword compiler by profession; his favourite possession is a bound volume of the Petit Larousse dictionary which sits prominently on his desk. He is prone to rants about competitors who, according to him, bend the rules of crossword making. It usually starts off quietly, as he first carefully examines his own technique:

"Comma ça, c'est juste. C'est correcte. C'est en ordre."

But things soon heat up when he examines the wrong way to do things, as exemplified by a rival, often building to a crescendo of insults:

"Putain de merde! Il est fou! Il est completement fou, quoi!"

But all of this is helping my understanding of French; I am learning fast, now that it's the only language spoken around me. Contrary to my expectations, Jeanot and Gabrielle live in a small flat with two children, and I have the sofa bed. Their recent accommodation of the brass band is more a sign of generosity than of any real capacity; the group would have completely covered the living room floor.

I catch a lift into town every morning with Gabrielle's commute and resume my regular visits to the agency, until one day, after a whole week of their kind hospitality, I finally get offered a posting.

And so it emerges that my first ever paid work will be at a motorbike spare parts distributer. The floor manager, who barks out commands in incomprehensible French, at first thinks me stupid when I fail to react in the appropriate manner. But there is help at hand from Pete, an American co-worker of similar age, who, like me, is working for the agency. He shows me the ropes, and I quickly get the hang of it; it's repetitive work, requiring the collation of orders from various boxes around the warehouse - a cable here, a gasket there - and we each get through hundreds of these every day. I have never been on my feet before for eight hours a day, and the desperate urge to sit down is hard to bear beyond even the first hour. After a few days I develop blisters and athlete's foot. It's an unpleasant initiation.

But Pete turns out to be a saviour in similar vein to Jeanot. He has worked the summer in Geneva before and knows of a better posting we can get through the agency. He negotiates on my behalf, and we are put on a waiting list. And finally, after three weeks of relentlessly pounding the warehouse floor, we are reassigned to the waterworks ...

Spanning one half of the Rhone, five bridges down from the lake, lies the waterworks building of Geneva. As the river passes through its arches, the water is pumped out and filtered for drinking. In the summer months, however, the lake becomes filled with grass cuttings from the surrounding hills, and this in turn clogs the grates of the waterworks. Dressed in light blue overalls that look and feel more like a comfortable pair of pyjamas, our job is to rake out the grass and deposit it into chutes which line a walkway suspended from the side of the building. The work is physically tiring, but nevertheless much more satisfying than the repetitive pacing of the warehouse. Better still, the grates need cleaning only twice a day, morning and afternoon, and for rest of the day we are sent on gardening duties.

The summer schedule of grass cutting requires a journey to the various water substations around Geneva, and so to some of the prettiest parts of the canton. The weather is sunny and pleasant, and it's good to be outside. Often we are left unsupervised and can spend a few lazy hours raking grass until we are picked up. The rest of the crew come from Italy and Yugoslavia, and are generally a lot older than us; seasonal workers with weather-beaten faces who come to do the jobs that the Swiss don't want to do. And we all talk our own brand of pidgin French to each other, something that is far easier for me to understand. In fact, after several weeks, I even start thinking to myself in this simplified language involuntarily; it's an odd sensation, as if my subconscious is engaged in repetitive practice so that I can speak it more freely when required.

The summer passes peacefully in this way, with the simplicity of a routine that has fallen into step with those around me. I have found a better room close to work, complete with sunny balcony, and there is a social life with Pete and his friends that is enough to keep me occupied. Most of all I am enjoying the physical work. There is a simple equation that is immensely satisfying: I work hard, I eat well, I sleep, I get paid. And at the end of the day there is money left over to spend in another place and another time. It is this pattern of save and spend that will serve me well in the future, as I begin to appreciate the freedom of choice that it gives me.

Towards the end of my stay, I am taken aside by an Italian at the waterworks who has found something in the grates. He shows me a large bundle of plastic straws wrapped in thick rubber bands.

"C'est la drogue?" he asks me.

"Je sais pas," I reply, but I tell him I can find out.

It transpires that the railing next to the waterworks is a well known haunt for drug dealers who dispose of their merchandise in the river whenever the police turn up unexpectedly. This particular one has been caught on the grate. Pete confirms to me that it is cannabis oil, with each straw containing a unit for sale; there are fifty in all. I buy the whole package from the Italian for a few banknotes, and we are all happy with the deal. But with little time left in my stay to smoke what could be as much as a years supply, I take a risk that only the young could possibly take.

In a scene reminiscent of the first five minutes of 'Midnight Express', I go into the men's toilets at Geneva airport half an hour before my flight to London. The package, conveniently phallic in shape, is stuffed down the front of my pants. I have reasoned that no one will expect drugs to be brought to London from Geneva. And to my relief, when I walk through the green channel at Heathrow airport later that day, I am proved entirely correct ...

After a long summer of busking that takes in everything from the London Underground to the promenade at Cannes in the South of France, the arrival of autumn signals a return to my studies.

It is common knowledge that Oxford bestows on its students a prestige that comes more from reputation than from education. It is an association by name only, and it is enough for most to have merely attended and completed their course. I had been told that for those with ambition, the top ten percent could achieve a first class degree by working exceptionally hard; however, there is a risk of failure with this strategy, and the middle eighty percent could get a second or third without too much effort. And it is with this combination of cynicism and practicality that I decide to approach my time at university.

In the first year, I stop going to lectures after only a few weeks; they are rushed, tedious and uninspiring, and the subjects themselves are mostly abstract and unappealing. I copy the course work from my obliging fellow students, and the only commitment I have each week are two one hour sessions with my tutors. It allows me to do other things, and I spend a lot of time rehearsing the band and visiting my girlfriend in London. My favourite clothes now are the light blue overalls of the waterworks, which I wear like a badge of honour, and I still indulge with abandon the new found pleasures of alcohol.

But the situation comes to a head in the summer when I am threatened with expulsion from the university; someone has noticed that I am not participating. Summoned before a board of governors, I duly promise to repent my ways and return to the lecture hall. Subsequently, I have a surreal experience with one of my tutors that is typical of our relationship. I have submitted coursework in which I solve a problem with simple logic, rather than the application of mathematical theories that the course required. The single sheet of paper rests conspicuously on the desk between us, and he sits in silence, not uttering a word. I respond to this with my own defiant silence, until finally the hour is up, and I leave.

As a result of all this unwelcome attention, I decide to revise hard for the first year exams, spending three weeks of intensive study to get up to date. Thoroughly prepared, and with a little luck with the questions, I pass the exam easily, scoring the highest mark of the six students in my tutorial group; the governors are off my back, as is my tutor, and the next two years will be an easy ride ...

In the summer of 1982 I return to Geneva, but this time I have planned ahead. Firstly I have secured an apartment in the centre of the old town with the help of a Swiss-Italian I befriended on my last visit; I will sublet from a friend of his who is away for the summer. I have also managed to line up a job at the agency, having forewarned them of my arrival. And soon there is a third and final string to my bow. After two weeks struggling with a difficult commute to my workplace on the edge of town, I have been generously offered the use of a Vespa by a co-worker. And now, with my own two wheels in true Italian style and a place in the chicest part of town, I can look forward to a full summer's work at the Geneva sewage works.

The work here is reminiscent of the waterworks, with cleaning taking place at the beginning and end of the day, and gardening filling in the gaps. However, the nature of the cleaning is quite different. In the morning

I put on thigh-high wellington boots and, armed with a brush, scrub the channels that take the raw sewage into the plant. Every day the three sides of this trough become covered with a thin and ominously brown layer; the task of removing this from the four hundred yards of waterways takes two hours and is back straining work. The smell is foul, but not overwhelmingly so. Then at the end of the day the aerated pools need to be cleaned in similar fashion; a crust that forms on the sides has to be washed off with fireman hoses. There are seven pools, and two of us work from the outside in, meeting at the centre with a customary water fight. The hoses are powerful and dangerous - score a direct hit, and you will knock someone over; let go of it, and the hose will spin around mercilessly spraying all and sundry. Unfortunately, the mist produced by all this water spray eventually gets inhaled, and at the end of the day there is an unpleasant tang of excrement that lingers at the back of my throat ...

But with a large part of the day spent gardening, it is easy work, and I am soon used to the smell and taste of the place. I have visitors from London who stay at my flat, and I enjoy a long summer of independence once again in my adopted city.

And there is one moment to be proud of before I return to England. Towards the end of my time at the sewage works, I am asked to help out in another part of the plant. There is a small room at the back where all the solids are collected from the water and transferred by overhead pipe into a waiting truck, ready to be transported to a landfill. The process is untidy, and some of it spills out onto the road, whereupon I am duly handed a spade to clean up the mess. And now I can say that I have actually done it: I have shovelled shit for a living.

10. shit jobs

How can we understand that strange beast ambition? What makes us choose those particular inspirations which, tempered by self-knowledge, serve to guide us? In my late teens and early twenties I would often imagine my younger self meeting my older self. It was a conceit that allowed me to step out of the page whilst engaged in a speculative scripting of my life. And for me there was always one common theme in those expectations: I imagined that person to have done something different with his life, to be something a little out of the ordinary; to have, at the very least, a story to tell. It was as if I wanted to shake off the comfortable suburban ordinariness of my youth. There was no other defining ambition, certainly no desire to be an actuary or accountant as my degree might qualify me, or to be rich by any means, as was common amongst my fellow students. To me, materialism seemed more likely to burden than to liberate. I did, however, possess a creative compulsion which, though stifled in education, had been reborn in music; but that particular ray of hope shone only briefly before flickering and extinguishing itself in the embers of bruised egos. I had been in four different bands during my time at Oxford, and all had petered out. Though enjoyable, they had lacked the necessary mix of talent and drive to make them succeed.

And so, when I graduate in the summer of 1984, one thing I am sure of is what I will not be doing: there will be no submission of CVs to graduate fairs, no filling in of applications to join corporations large or small. For there is no ambition whatsoever in this regard. Instead, I decamp to a room in my mother's house near Kingston. And in the absence of any clear guiding light, I amble down to the job centre one fine summer's day and take the first offer that comes my way. Despite my recently acquired Oxford degree, my first paid work in England will be a job as a dustman.

'On the dust', as it is known colloquially, turns out to be a rigorous and exhausting role, a perfect antidote to my recent sedentary studies. I am assigned to a route that covers an eclectic mix of council estates and millionaire's mansions in Kingston upon Thames. The crew that I work with are motivated solely by speed; the sooner we finish the circuit, the sooner we can go home. We start at 7 a.m. and jog round the streets to keep up with the unrelenting advance of the dustcart. They have it timed to perfection, like a military exercise, with a twenty minute break for breakfast in the middle. With this energetic approach, we are usually finished before lunch. But it's backbreaking work. Most of the bins in the estates are made of galvanised steel and are often filled to the brim with rain sodden waste and maggots - there are no removable plastic liners, all bins must be carried to the cart, emptied and returned. The regulars carry two at a time on their backs, and I am keen to match their feats whenever I can. After a few weeks, I develop mountainous biceps that look completely out of place on my skinny frame.

There is a small amount of time for banter, during the breakfast break, or on the drive to and from the depot. They are proud of their short working day and wonder if I have aspirations to be full-time on the job.

"You got any qualifications mate?" they ask.

"Er .. I got one 'O' level," I say, testing the water.

"Bloody 'ell! Brain of Britain! What you doin' 'ere?" one of them says. I should have aimed a bit lower.

At other times there are moments that shock me and do not enamour me to them at all. There are not many black faces in this part of London, but when they see one walking by the side of the road there is a torrent of abuse. It's vicious and full of hatred for a stranger they have never met.

I get moved from crew to crew each week, working holiday cover for all the different routes, and I never really relax into any form of routine. When I am finally let go at the end of the summer, I have really only achieved two things: firstly, I have never been fitter and stronger; and secondly, I have just found a room to rent nearer the centre of town, through an ex-band-member. I am moving to Balham.

One aspect of this experience is proving to be encouraging: I am finding work easily, without the need to resort to my qualifications. To embark on a career now would require a long term commitment of mind and spirit that

I am not yet prepared for. And so it is that I wander, ambitionless once more, down to the local job centre, this time in Tooting.

I should describe myself now, as I sit waiting for an interview at the Ministry of Defence. Gone are the light blue overalls of the waterworks, and in their place is a donkey jacket, grey jeans and army boots, topped with peroxide Mohican and dagger earrings. It was not my intention to be dressed this way for an interview, but I was sent directly from the job centre. The brigadier, dressed in old-fashioned tweeds, seems unperturbed, however; he appears to take a liking to me and surprisingly offers me the job. The post itself has been loftily described as 'sound engineer, grade 5 experimental worker', but it turns out to be something slightly less than inspirational.

My place of work is an ordinary looking warehouse in South London which houses a large collection of books; it is in essence a library. British soldiers based in West Germany request books from here, which are duly sent out to their base. But they may also request tapes, essentially recordings of radio programmes broadcast in the UK by the BBC. My job is to programme a timer to record these radio transmissions day and night, then make a designated number of copies. My office is equipped with four high speed tape copying machines and a state of the art music system. Most of the day is spent listening to the radio and chatting with my fellow operatives who are engaged in more bureaucratic duties. The people I work with are in the civil service, and the prevailing attitude is one of smugness, something born from an ingrained belief in their own job security; I am welcomed into the fold like a lucky guest to their private party. But there is, nevertheless, a nervous tension beneath the surface, a fear that someone is about to become wise to their situation and reallocate their services. For this particular building is in the process of downsizing, and already strange things are afoot next door ...

On the warehouse floor, amongst the aisles of bookracks, are a team of workers busy about their task; they move slowly from shelf to shelf, taking weeks to complete their operations on each row. For unfortunately, almost half of these books have been designated out of date and are now doomed for destruction. Not unreasonably, the ones chosen for termination are those that have been left neglected and unrequested for many years; it is a necessary cull. However, there is one small matter making this process a lengthy one. The team must take each book and carefully tear one of its pages out before it is removed. In an apparent effort to avoid adverse publicity, the source of these books, destined to be burnt somewhere, must never be known. And so, like removing teeth from a corpse, the identifying library stamp is torn from each book one by one, so that in the ashes of their clandestine resting place, there will be not one shred of evidence remaining.

Meanwhile, despite being contracted for only six months to do this job, I am struggling to maintain my enthusiasm for the task. Every morning I am faced with the same long day filled with very little to do. I am seated all the time, stupefied by the small talk, and the best thing that can be hoped for is the odd interesting show on Radio Four. There is nothing to tax me mentally or physically, and as the winter draws in and the days become shorter, the hours seem to stretch further into the night. But I have come up with a plan in this vacuum. I have been considering going travelling since my band fell apart last year, but up to this time I had no particular destination in mind. Now a friend has told me of an acquaintance who recently crossed the Sahara Desert, saying it was possible to get lifts with the many car runners who travel that route. It is enough to make my mind up. After 3 months of sound engineer grade 5 experimental duty, I quit ...

The months following my return from West Africa were difficult times, full of introspection and half-hearted attempts at resurrecting the band. There was a period of signing on the dole, followed by a procession of odd jobs: photocopying for an accounts department, cleaning at a private maternity clinic, packing at an electronics firm, building work excavating a basement. But soon I stumbled onto something far more suitable to my disposition. I got a job driving a van.

'White van man', as he is known, has a reputation for being an overly aggressive driver, and I soon find out why. Working from a distribution centre that delivers drug supplies to chemists, I am required to stop at thirty separate locations on my route before lunch, and then the same thirty after. To make this work in the time frame, I have to leave the engine running while I sprint into the store carrying all the packages. Anything considered a dangerous drug, such as morphine, is kept in a padlocked box which slows you down even further. Like being on the dust, you are free to go home when you finish the afternoon run, so the urge to drive quickly is even more pressing. But aside from the odd broken wing mirror, there is never any real danger to my driving; just a determined impatience to get to the next place as quickly as possible.

And there is something else that I have discovered. I like being on the road. There is a sense of time passing that is lacking in other types of manual work; this one demands concentration for the most part, and has flurries of physical activity to break the monotony. Above all there is no boss to look over, no pressure applied other than your own. And it is far easier in this environment to exist however you wish to in your own head ...

Later in the summer, I return to Oxford on a promise of free lodging in a house vacated for the holidays. With my newly found profession I register with a local driving agency, who quickly assign me to the local authority that care for the elderly. My job is to tow a mobile chiropody clinic around the quaint villages of Oxfordshire, a task that I am taking over from a retiree before a suitable replacement can be found. The clinic is a large grey prefab on wheels, the length of two caravans, and is hitched to the back of a Land Rover that pulls it furtively along the small country lanes of the Cotswolds. In each village I set up the clinic in a car park or lay-by, then prepare it for the day; in the afternoon, I dismantle everything and tow it to the next village. There is little to do in between but ferry a number of old people to and from the clinic. Unfortunately I cannot shake off my 'white van man' mentality; my driving is fast and urgent, and the pensioners often emerge pale faced from the back seat of the Land Rover.

The afternoons are mostly empty, and I make use of the car to run my own private errands around town. But at the end of each day, I find myself once more at the lower end of my taste threshold. The work that has been done in the clinic is a messy affair, and littering the floor now are the offcuts and surpluses to all those elderly feet - yellowing toenails, calluses and corns; all manner of dead skin must now be swept up carefully and disposed of. It continues a trend of nauseous chores that seem destined to blight my existence.

Next I am assigned to a plumbers merchant, delivering spare parts door to door; and soon after that, a private security firm that has branched out into parcel deliveries. Both of these introduce me to 'three tonners', a lorry large enough to carry heavy loads, yet small enough to be driven legally without a heavy goods license. They are surprisingly easy to drive, though the air brakes require a delicate touch to avoid being thrown violently against the windscreen. And despite being bigger and heavier, the manner in which they are driven sticks closely to the white van man book of rules.

The plumbing job takes me once again all over the beautiful Oxfordshire countryside, this time to remote farmsteads where a replacement cistern or copper pipe may be required. In contrast, the parcel route is confined to the drab industrial estates that surround the town; it is, however, a quick circuit, which allows me to sleep comfortably in the cab for a few hours at lunchtime. And I have learnt another important lesson on this job from my fellow workers; never mark your parcel as fragile, or it will be thrown with even more force into the back of the truck.

But with cheap lodgings easy to find, and an old Mini van bought for a song to provide me wheels, there is a simple existence that I am falling into. It is in this setting that I embark on my next journey to East Africa, and then, six months later, a third journey to Thailand. From a disjointed beginning to my post educational life, I am settling into a routine and an identity of sorts. In fact I am two things right now. I am a delivery driver and I am a traveller.

the conveyor belt

What can we make of this sorry tale of impoverished ambition?

How much advantage, how much opportunity can one man accumulate year on year, hence to be thrown so carelessly away?
And what of the benefactors - the taxpayers and parents whose hard earned funds are so ruthlessly squandered?
How can they not feel outrageously cheated?

And yet perhaps this is something far worse than the mere counting of pounds and pennies that might be lost in one failed enterprise or another.
For how can we measure that attribute so often judged the least utilised of all, that intangible thing we call talent?
Of one thing we can be absolutely sure: there is very little used in those aimless pursuits so eloquently catalogued here.

Yet all is in place for him. A conveyor belt, built and serviced by our predecessors, is ready, polished and gleaming, to carry him forward like thousands of others to a bright and promising future. He has been chosen, groomed and prepared. And all is set but for one small thing - he stubbornly refuses to step on.

And see how low he sinks! Can one go lower than a sewage farmer, a rubbish collector, a sweeper of calluses and corns?
No. It is clear. This can only be seen as a blatant two fingered salute to the world; and in particular to those who hold the upstanding values of education and privilege as a gateway to their future.

But with this condemnation there should also be attempts at understanding. For is it not in our interest to learn from such anomalies, such blips in the order of things?

Where was the vocational inspiration necessary for one so young to find a direction in life? How amongst the abstraction of ones studies can a willing student see fruitful application or meaning of any sort?

For this fast changing world they enter has often moved on from the one they have been prepared for. It may be as well to start their real education there ...

And regarding this reliable conveyor belt, surely there is one more choice beyond the simple yin yang position? To step on and off when desired can also be considered ...

For this particular man is a product of his times - a prosperous time of cheap travel and easy employment. Who would not exploit such opportunity given half a chance?

But to work in labour, in the lowest and dirtiest of jobs?

This I propose to be an honourable endeavour, and perhaps one that the rich and privileged of this world should be compelled to experience. For how much more important it is for the rich to know the poor, than for the poor to know the rich ...

Yet still there are some who will say:
Why stoop so low? What kind of life is that?

And I respectfully respond: on the contrary.
It could even be said: what kind of life this is!

11. moscow

The train pulls into Yaroslavsky station in the north east of Moscow early on a warm and sunny Tuesday morning. It has been six days since we left Beijing, and now we must bid farewell to our Russian battle-axe as the Trans-Siberian leg of our journey reaches its final stop. The time for reflection has passed, and we can be tourists once again.

Moscow is a historic city, and although we have only been issued with a two day transit visa, we plan to use as much of our quota as possible. While we book our onward travel for the following night at the ticket office, we learn that there is a designated waiting room where foreign transit passengers can sleep; there are no cheap rooms available in town, only high end hotels that require payment in foreign currency. Quickly depositing our belongings in a baggage check, we set off for the nearest metro station.

Unbeknown to us, the Moscow underground is famous for its ornate decor, each station having its own distinctive architectural style, from Classical to Stalinist to Art Deco. We descend the crowded escalator transfixed, passing beneath chandeliers and elaborate murals, like the entrance to a secret underground palace. Soon our spell is broken by the harsh Russian voice of a tannoy, and all eyes turn towards us simultaneously. It appears we have been spotted by an eagle-eyed supervisor from her vantage point at the top of the stairs: we are standing on the wrong side of the escalator. We wave to her obligingly, noting an uncanny resemblance to our recently departed battle-axe; she seems to be everywhere ...

After five stops on the train we find ourselves at Red Square. It is in this famous open space that, only a year ago, a West German pilot landed his Cessna plane, breaching the Soviet air defence and causing widespread panic. And now we discover that this day too has its own share of history. For the first time in fourteen years, there is a U.S. presidential visit to Moscow - Ronald Reagan is in town. Perhaps this should be inconsequential to us, but it turns out to be somewhat problematic. Although we are still flush with roubles, alcohol is nowhere to be found.

Our usual suppliers, the street kids who swap jeans and tapes, have run out because all the vodka outlets have been closed down; it transpires that, in order to avoid a bad press from all the foreign journalists flying in for the summit, drunks have been removed from the streets and their supplies hastily cut off. The whole of Moscow is in a state of prohibition.

But this has only increased our determination to christen our arrival with a celebratory drink. We walk for hours through the long wide avenues of the city, admiring the classical European architecture that emerged relatively unscathed from the second world war, but with one eye looking out for a bar or a shop that might serve our needs. Finally we stumble across a small group gathering down one of the side streets. There seems to be a queue forming, and although we cannot see beyond the door through which it snakes, we have time on our hands and curiosity in abundance.

"Vodka?" we ask, expecting that the word requires no translation.

The man next in line shrugs as if to say: maybe, maybe not. But like all queues, the assumption must be made that something worthwhile awaits us at the other end. And so it turns out when we finally reach the end of the line. Rationing is still enforced in Russia, and we are duly sold our strict allowance from today's special consignment. We emerge from the store triumphant, each of us carrying our own hard earned bottle of Russian champagne.

We decamp hastily to a park bench near Revolution Square to drink our spoils. Unfortunately the first bottle is a little lively; the cork shoots twenty feet into the air and with astonishing accuracy strikes a policeman's head on its way down. We are quickly admonished and ordered to move on; but it's a half-hearted rebuke, and the bottle is drunk less conspicuously under a nearby tree.

Here in the centre of town, Moscow feels like any other European city. There is a buzz about the place, and the people are outside enjoying the hot summer's day. Lining the squares are vending machines that for a few small coins will dispense refreshing cold drinks. A glass is supplied that is reused by the next customer by washing under a tap. It sells lemonade and kvass, a kind of watered down beer which is perfect to quench our thirst. And all around us are tourist kiosks selling statues and badges of Lenin and Stalin, in the same way that miniature Eiffel Towers might be sold in Paris.

In the evening we find a restaurant in one of the railway stations. It's a grand affair, similar in style to the metro stations, with a cavernous roof from which intricate glass chandeliers are suspended over each dining table. With roubles still to burn, we order a four course meal washed down with the obligatory Russian champagne kept on ice. It is a much anticipated feast, and in luxurious contrast to the accommodation we will soon retire to: the thinly carpeted floor of a waiting room, which we will soon share with twenty or so others.

The next day we walk further along the beautiful avenues of the city and in the afternoon join yet another queue, this time with full knowledge of what lies at the end. After a long wait, we are ushered in to a dimly lit room where Vladimir Lenin lies in state for all the world to see. Although somewhat macabre, it is hard not to be fascinated by this apparition; I have rarely come across a dead body, yet laid out in front of me is one of the most important politicians in history, suited and bearded, and almost perfectly preserved. And as we pay our respects to Lenin in a suitably dignified fashion, we are aware too that the time is coming for us to bid farewell to Moscow. Just one last meal in our favourite restaurant awaits, before we board the late night train to Berlin ...

After two days crossing western Russia and Poland, we reach the East German border as night falls. It is not far from there to Berlin, which sits geographically in the centre of East Germany with a narrow motorway corridor connecting it to its counterpart West Germany. In a strange appendix to the second world war, both Germany and Berlin were carved up into four arbitrary parts for the Soviets, Americans, British and French; the cold war in the fifties then gave rise to a concrete wall, which now separates East from West Berlin.

The train stops just before we reach the wall, and this time a thorough search of the train is undertaken with sniffer dogs. The East German border guards who sweep through the carriages are reminiscent of the second world war with their Teutonic looks, smart uniforms, and abrupt commands barked in a harsh German rasp. It is hard not to imagine someone stowed away under a seat somewhere in a desperate bid for freedom. After a clean sweep, the train crawls onwards through the eerily dark and silent eastern suburbs, before crossing the wall just north of Checkpoint Charlie. We have arrived in the West.

And it is not just the bright street lamps and neon signs that signal our transition to a different world. Having arrived too late to collect the keys to our apartment, we ask some locals at the station for directions to a cheap hotel; they respond with an invitation to sleep on their floor. This offer is made so easily, that it is hard not to be impressed by the hospitality of these young Berliners. Their apartment proves to be more than comfortable, as too does the one we move into the next day, so generously lent to us by that friend of Stacey's that we barely even met.

And now we have another historic European city to explore. This time we are more interested in the subculture of the city, a product of the disproportionately large presence of young people who support various anti-war and anti-eastern-block political movements. Frankie, the Berliner I met in West Africa, had told me that this city is a magnet for conscientious objectors like himself, who can avoid the German national service by being registered here. We visit an area of town camped out by squatters and punks near an exposed section of the wall. Colourful murals adorn the sides of terraced housing, while graffiti fills the length of the wall like a modern art installation stretching to infinity. There are tents and stalls, and an atmosphere of peaceful demonstration similar to an open air music festival, though here they are a permanent fixture. In a year from now, I will watch the destruction of the Berlin wall on television with disbelief, and I will imagine this place to be the exact spot where the first hammer blows are struck.

And whilst in Berlin, we do what the Germans do even better than the Dutch or the British: we drink beer. After almost two weeks of vodka and champagne, it is something we indulge in heartily; here the beer is strong and served in litre jugs, often adorned with a bearded Bavarian dancing in lederhosen to remind us of its traditional home. Yet whilst we try hard to enjoy this respite from the rice beer of Eastern Asia, there is something preying on both our minds. Home is not far away, and our friends and families are now closer in our thoughts; we will not be spending too long in this town.

After three days, I bid farewell to Kurt, as he sets off to catch a train to Amsterdam. We have resolved to meet up soon, and hopefully go travelling together again. I take a local bus to the edge of the city and start hitchhiking; I have heard of someone who once hitched all the way to London from Berlin, and I am keen to match his feat. After four hours of holding up a 'London' sign and watching all around me get lifts to more reasonable targets, a car finally stops for me just at the moment I am giving up hope. A young German in a Karmann Ghia hastily makes room in the passenger seat, and drives me all the way across Germany to a village in Holland; arriving late at night, I am offered dinner and a bed at his aunt's house. The conversation we have during those four long hours of driving is cathartic; to tell my story to a stranger and to hear his life story in return, each of us a willing and captive audience, brings a small but renewed comfort in humanity.

After breakfast the next day, he takes me to a motorway slip road where I soon get a lift to Rotterdam, and from there a ferry to Dover. I haven't quite hitched all the way to London, but I've had an interesting and eventful journey nevertheless. All that remains for me now is to face the unknown; a blank canvas stretching ahead of me once more, with no discernible outline to follow. And as this long journey comes to an end, closing another chapter in my life, the voice in my head is offering me no real clues or insights; like the East Berlin I have just travelled through, there is only a dark and eery silence.

reflection

What great fortune it is to have such times in your life to reflect and take stock! How important it is to make way for it!

Yet how few people, when burdened with the day to day or hand to mouth, can say with all honesty that this is something they possess?
How many of us will keep marching onwards with no real grasp of the where or the why?

And as this wandering misfit returns to that great well of opportunity that awaits him in his prosperous homelands, what conclusion will be reached from this precious gift of reflection?
To return to the fold? To join the throng? To step back on?

He will not. For this aimless soul is as restless as ever.
Where has been the great revelation? Where the new calling? Where the irresistible urge to become a man of material wealth?

There is none. For the bite from the bug that bit is now more infectious than ever. This strange nomadic compulsion has become an almighty force, spurred on by the countless tales told by the legions of the likewise afflicted.

There will be more continents to see, more cultures to absorb and many more stories to be told before this curiosity can finally be laid to rest ...

PART 2

12. watamu

It's 1991, and I am living in Watamu, a small village lying next to the Indian ocean on the Kenyan coast. The house I am renting sits on a rocky promontory overlooking a beach of rare and distinct natural beauty. Scattering the bay are small mushroom shaped outcrops, topped with green scrub, which at low tide merge with a vast honeycombed plain to resemble a collection of woodlands and trees carved crudely out of coral rock. During the day this stunning landscape is slowly transformed by the incoming tide to create an altogether different spectacle - a sea of magical floating islands.

Yet despite the idyllic nature of my surroundings, I have the feeling once again that I am stuck, not only between one place and another, but also perhaps between fantasy and reality. For on the one hand, I am waiting for someone - a fellow traveller I have arranged to meet before we head off to India; and on the other hand, I am living in Watamu as part of a family. In this small breeze-block house overlooking the sea, I am sharing a room with my African girlfriend Jamila and her four year old son Otto.

It was a long chain of events that brought me here. Six months earlier, I had met an Englishman, Neil, in a small budget hotel in Cairo. Both of us at loose ends, we hatched a plan for an epic journey that would take us through Sudan to Central Africa. However, a breakout of war in southern Sudan had soon put paid to that idea, and we had been forced instead to fly direct to Nairobi; from there we planned to travel onwards through Uganda and Zaire. We were in no real hurry, and after a week camping in the Masai Mara, we decided on a trip to the coast before setting off on our longer journey. Neil, having recently learnt to scuba dive in the Red Sea, saw an opportunity to add more experience to his diving log; and I could see no reason to protest.

To this end Watamu has a dive school at the Turtle Bay resort, and as we alight from the matatu that drops us in the centre of the village, we are met by a tout peddling rooms for the night. In normal circumstance we would head straight for a cheap hotel, but this time our curiosity is piqued by his suggestion that a house is available for rent. This particular house turns out to be ideally placed, with a garden gate opening straight onto the beach, and a terrace raised just high enough to get a clear view of those teetering mushroom islands. Luckily we are able to negotiate a nominal rent; the owner is an ex-pat who lives in Nairobi, and it is his resourceful servants who let the house without his knowledge.

The diving is good. After training in a swimming pool for a few days, I join up with Neil to go deep sea diving on a reef about a mile offshore. We dive without the cumbersome wetsuits and stabiliser jackets normally required; the water is warm, and we ascend and descend using the buoyancy of our lungs. For someone who has never experienced diving before, it's a revelation; it feels like being suspended in the air, floating through a surreal and alien landscape. We see stone fish, scorpion fish and moray eels, and chase an octopus as it squirts us with ink. On my second dive we spot a large manta ray circling, and I am able to swim underneath it for tens of yards at almost touching distance. At this point I can say without reservation that I am hooked.

In the evenings we sample the local nightspots, and it's at one of the more upmarket of these that I meet Jamila for the first time. There is an instant attraction between us, and of course I'm perfectly set up to invite her back to our 'villa' for a nightcap on the terrace. She is on a night out with a friend who has taken a liking to Neil, but which unfortunately is not in the least part reciprocated; she tags along anyway, perhaps still hopeful that Neil will see her differently through drunken eyes.

Jamila is twenty-six to my twenty-nine and works as a cook in one of the many camps of tourist bungalows that line the outskirts of Watamu. The existence of her son Otto is only revealed to me on our third date, but by then I am expecting as much, after her friend confided this to me in an apparent fit of jealousy. The initial effect of this news is one of elevated responsibility, as if this newly born relationship has taken on a more serious tone by this mere fact. But this feeling is exacerbated when I finally meet him. For Otto is not at face value a normal child. Of mixed race, his features show traces of downs syndrome, and he appears to suffer from a severe lack of development; at four years old he is still in nappies, and has not yet learnt to walk or talk.

A short time after this poignant introduction, my newly found hobby comes back to bite me in the form of a near death experience. At twenty-five metres deep, I find myself struggling to equalise the pressure in my ears - when I go up, the pain increases; when I go down, it increases further still. Eventually my left eardrum bursts. As my head goes into a dizzying spin, I am acutely aware of the danger of passing out; the sensation is not unlike the one you might experience from standing up too quickly, but this time the world that spins around me is a watery one. I can see the instructor swimming away from me and no other divers in sight. But resisting the urge to panic, I wait for the slow trickle of warm water into my inner ear to cease and the world to come back into sharper focus. Still dangerously light-headed, I swim slowly towards him and give the distress signal.

It is my fondest memory of Neil that when we surface, his anger is so plain to see:

"Why did we come up? That's fifteen quid wasted on a five minute dive!"

"I nearly drowned," I reply stonily, but he remains less than convinced.

In fact the incident leads to a nasty ear infection that needs treatment from a specialist in Mombasa. What emerges from my ear in the doctor's tweezers is a bloody lump the size of two marbles. The consequence for me is an eardrum that will forever distort the wail of an ambulance or the scream of a child like a torn loud speaker.

And after three weeks of healing, the time eventually comes for us to continue on our travels. I have considered the idea of Jamila coming with us, but it would be far too difficult with Otto in tow. And so I bid an emotional farewell to both of them, and Neil and I set off as planned for the Ugandan border ...

It would be a further three months before I would find my way back to Watamu. Neil and I eventually parted ways on a passenger boat travelling the length of Lake Tanganyika, he heading south to Namibia to find work diving for diamonds, and I disembarking in Tanzania to return to my recently adopted family.

The house where we live now on the promontory is small and sparse, the three of us sleeping in one room, while the African owner sleeps in the other. Although the sheets are clean, both the mattress and pillows have the musky smell of old sweat, soaked up from its previous occupants and preserved by the constant humidity. Jamila cooks on the floor of the kitchen with a small charcoal stove, but only the simpler fare such as tea and toast, or beans for Otto. For the rest we eat in the village, where the local staple is fish and rice or sausage and chips. And every morning I try to spot the boy who roams the streets and alleyways selling copies of the Kenyan Gazette, an English language newspaper with a simple digest of news that keeps me connected to the world. I am used to the life here now, and my face is becoming known amongst the locals.

Although there are a number of hotels and resorts in Watamu, at its heart is an African village, whose eclectic mix of Kenyan tribes and Somali refugees are all hustling for something. The women are the boldest, often asking me for money:

"Give me ten shillings," one says, holding her hand out to me as I walk past.

"Why?" I ask rhetorically.

"Because you have money and I don't," she hazards.

"I already have a family to look after, thanks."

"You want to fuck me too? You can fuck me too."

There are perhaps cultural differences at work here; it is common for African men to have more than one wife. And the same simple logic confronts me in the evenings when I am drinking in the local African bars; whether Jamila is with me or not, I am always asked to buy beer for the women of the village. Although I do not feel like a rich tourist from one of the nearby resorts, I do nevertheless wear the same badge as them, a pale white face. And in this coexistence of rich and poor or white and black, I straddle both sides in my relationship with Jamila; we are not one nor the other, but something apart.

Every day now, I practice walking and talking with Otto. His first word after "mama" is "ball", something that I bought for him along with a xylophone and toy trumpet. It is slow progress, but feels significant nonetheless. When I first met him he was walking on all fours, but now he is able to walk short distances down the beach with only one hand holding mine. It is hard at this point to judge the severity of his disability. On the one hand, his appearance would suggest a genetic disorder, but on the other, he has lacked an environment conducive to development. For most of his life he has been left with minders while Jamila worked, women who speak different tribal languages and pay no real attention to the seventh or eighth child in their charge.

It is a tragic story for him. Otto's German father disowned him at birth when seeing him for the first time. He ordered two blood tests, refusing to believe the baby was his. His wife is a rich American, a high flying diplomat who works at the U.S. embassy in Mogadishu, and Otto the result of an affair on the side with a pretty young African who helped in the home. Jamila travelled to Kenya on his instruction, ostensibly to have an abortion, but then decided against it. She has struggled ever since with a meagre allowance that petered out after three years.

And now this complex web has me unwittingly in its hold. My attraction to Jamila goes beyond a casual fling or experimentation. To me her exoticism is intoxicating; her lithe body, the smell of her hair, her silky skin, all contribute to an overwhelming desire in me. And there is a simplicity and calmness about her outlook that is refreshing and easy; in many ways I feel I have come across the perfect foil for my own angst-ridden western neuroses. But as my emotional involvement becomes stronger with Jamila, and increasingly with Otto too, I am aware of an impending dilemma; it is becoming impossible to reconcile this fact with my plans to leave for India.

And so, in the midst of this day to day existence, I hatch another plan. It might be more accurate to describe it as a fantasy, however, for what is consuming me now is the thought of starting a business. If I could build a small travellers hotel on a plot of land on the outskirts of Watamu, how much would it cost? Could the income pay back a loan? I remember with great clarity how Heiner had built his guest house on a beach in Borocay with his own hands; could I do the same here? The business could provide for my adopted family, perhaps a special education for Otto as well.

Even the architectural drawings have been carefully sketched on the front of a clean envelope. It will be a simple rectangular block with two stories - on the ground floor, twelve guest rooms will face outwards, six on each side; on the first floor, a bar and restaurant will afford distant views of the sea beneath an enormous thatched roof, with open walls to let the breeze through; and behind the bar will be the kitchen and owner's accommodation, a two bedroom suite. I have scouted the land, and the total cost that I calculate comes to the princely sum of twenty-thousand pounds. And that is where this particular exercise falters. For who would lend me such a sum? If I could think of someone with that kind of money to spare, would I even dare to ask?

The ever-circling thoughts of this dilemma soon bring to mind the last time I attempted to do business abroad. The experience was certainly an education, though the main lesson was one of trust. It took place two years ago in South America, on a journey I undertook shortly after my return from Moscow ...

13. the fourth journey

My fourth journey started on a simple enough premise. South America was a continent that inspired me for many reasons - as a region where the culture was similar to Europe, and thus where the conversation might flow as freely as the beer; as a continent with a wide variety of landscapes and natural beauty, from jungles and deserts to glaciers and volcanoes; and as an inexpensive place for adventure, where a well worn travellers circuit was already in place.

For budget has an important part to play in these decisions. I had worked overtime for six months as a delivery driver and sold two of my most precious possessions to pay for this trip - a Ludwig drum kit and a beaten up Mini van. Both were sold for a profit: the van an MOT failure which I fixed up on the cheap, and the drum kit bought from the small ads for far less than it was worth. Such are the small sums that make big differences in my life. It was enough to accumulate a critical mass of funds - nearly two thousand pounds, enough for a flight and about eight months of travelling.

I had also made a loose arrangement with Kurt to meet in Brazil in the new year; the plan was simple: I would find the best town for carnival, and he would fly out for the celebrations. And so, barely a month before Christmas, I set off on my own once more, this time with a one way ticket to Rio in my hand ...

It is no doubt true for most travellers that the shared experience of travelling accompanied is preferable to the lonely one. And as I leave the airport in Rio, I already find myself sharing a taxi with someone of similar age and disposition to me; his name is Marcus, and he's on a three month overland trip to Peru. After a few days acclimatising to the heat in Rio, he is ready to set off on his journey, and although his itinerary is somewhat rushed, I decide to take advantage of the opportunity and travel with him for at least part of the way.

I soon discover Brazil to be a country not only of big hearts, but also of big stomachs. As we travel south down the coast, we are often befriended by holidaying Brazilians who take us to see some of their favourite beaches or waterfalls. And this generosity of spirit is mirrored in the portions we are served for lunch in the bars and restaurants. On one occasion, as plate after plate arrives on our table - four pieces of chicken, six fish, a large bowl of rice, chips, beans, salad - I complain that we only ordered one portion between us, not two. Astonishingly, the waitress replies that it is indeed only one portion. When the bill arrives, it is for less than two dollars.

It is, however, hard to keep up with the price of things. Inflation here is out of control, and every business has its own blackboard on which the prices change daily. We have to exchange small denominations of dollars regularly to keep our spending on budget, although it is easy to find a shop or small business that will change on the black market. On the one occasion that I have to resort to a bank, I find the foreign exchange counter closed; instead the bank manager takes me into the back and gives me his own cash at the black market rate.

And after we have picked our way down the coastal resorts of Parati, whose cobbled streets and white stucco houses could come out of a Gabriel García Márquez novel, and Isla Bella, a rainforest island fringed by endless beaches, we take a panoramic train journey down to Paranagua called the Serra Verde express; it is a dizzying ride along a precipice clinging to the side of a mountain where you can hang out of the windows and look straight down. Marcus' itinerary so far has been carefully planned to take in the sights, and I am more than willing to let him be my guide. The next destination on my whistle-stop tour is Foz do Iguaçu, and it doesn't disappoint ...

The Iguaçu falls were only known to me from seeing them in the film 'The Mission', so there is nothing to prepare me for the massive scale of the site. The tops of the falls snake for three kilometres and fall onto two levels, like giant watery steps, the highest drop being over eighty metres. From the Brazilian side they are a stunning sight, but across the border in Argentina there is an altogether different perspective. It's a hot summer's day, and we find a place to bathe only a metre from the edge of the falls, where the cool waters are running slow. Floating on my back with a view looking over the precipice to the gorge below, it's a giddy moment.

Later we take the one kilometre walkway that spans the river at the top of the falls to the Devil's Throat. As befits the name, this is the horseshoe centre of the falls where the largest concentration of water cascades from all sides into one mist-filled chasm. Incredibly, a platform has been built teetering over the edge which allows a view straight down into the abyss below. The spectacle sucks you in both visually and emotionally. And as I stand there, an anxiety creeps in that I may somehow fall into its spell and jump, having lost all my will. It is certainly not a place to be feeling suicidal.

Back in town, I look to see if there are any letters waiting for me in the post office. Poste Restante is a service known to save the lives of travellers the world over, if not just for its morale boosting contact with loved ones, then for its ability to hold messages for fellow travellers. I had asked Kurt to write to me here, and sure enough a letter is waiting for me. But it's bad news: Kurt has had a series of setbacks in Amsterdam; one of his friends is back on heroin, another has overdosed, and his best friend and business partner has lost an eye in a bar fight. The latter problem in particular has curtailed his means of making money, and he can no longer afford to come out. It appears I am on my own.

With the obligation of waiting for Kurt now gone, I decide to keep up with Marcus' itinerary for a little while longer. Although he left for Paraguay the previous day, I am confident I can catch him up.

After a long bus ride I duly arrive in Asunción, the capital of this small landlocked country. It is a strange place, its streets teeming with South Korean traders selling all manner of electronic items for Christmas such as dancing Santas and singing Christmas cards, and an expat community that seem desperate for new faces to talk to. As a result, when I meet up with Marcus, we are invited to parties all over town by a group of English language teachers he has met in one of the bars downtown. Most of the evenings now are clouded in a toxic haze due to the potent mix of cocaine and alcohol we are bombarded with, and the nights seem to get longer and longer. At one party, we are introduced to a niece of President Stroessner. As Paraguay's long standing dictator of thirty-four years, he is famous for turning his country into a haven for drug smugglers, arms dealers and Nazi war criminals; he is also, like most South American dictators, suspected of suppressing and torturing any opposition to his power. Although we feel the need to choose our words carefully, she seems completely unaffected by this sinister family connection; she's just another girl out on the town.

But Marcus has a schedule that needs to be adhered to, and after four days we make a concerted effort to escape. We board a passenger boat travelling north along the Paraguai River, taking bunks in one of the inexpensive first class cabins. The name of this large vessel is, naturally, the Stroessner, and the two day journey proves to be sublimely relaxing, floating gently past the diverse birdlife of the Paraguayan marshes, as the river taking us slowly but surely towards our next port of call. For we are headed back to Brazil now. The next adventure on Marcus' tour will be a wetlands safari in the Pantanal ...

There is no waking vision in my life so far that can compare to what confronts me now. As my eyes slowly begin to focus through the early morning daze of a hangover, I am aware of a black shape on the floor, standing out from the light coloured tiling just a few yards from my hammock. I stare for a long time before I can register its identity. A large spider, six inches across. And it seems to be eating something. It's a tarantula eating vomit.

"Rambo!" I shout out groggily, "Tarantula!"

The spider is right underneath Rambo's hammock, where he must have thrown up last night after too much beer. Although his real name is Olaf, he insists on wearing a headband day and night; still sporting it now, he peers furtively over the edge of his hammock at the furry creature feasting on his regurgitated dinner. Minutes later, our guide is in the room, attacking the unfortunate spider with his shoe; forced to abandon its breakfast, it runs under the farmhouse to escape.

After it's gone, I head for the toilet for my usual early morning ablutions, locking myself inside the draughty outhouse. Something jumps out at me from the bowl.

"Aaagh!" I scream in panic. This time though, it's only a frog.

And yet this is what we are here for - the wildlife. We have seen giant guinea pigs called capybara, ocelots, monkeys throwing shit at us, all manner of birdlife, and most commonly the Yacare caiman, a type of alligator seven or eight feet long. Our guide demonstrates his courage by lassoing one with a rope and then, after a momentous struggle, turning it onto its back so that we can stroke its belly. At night we shine torches on the swamps to gauge their numbers and are met with hundreds of alligator eyes reflecting back at us ominously in the dark; there are apparently about ten million of them in the Pantanal alone.

On the last day of the tour, we fish for piranha. At first we entice them with raw chicken on a hook; then after the first few are caught, we cut them into pieces and use their own flesh as bait. The tug on the string is frenzied, and the teeth keep biting long after they're pulled from the river. During this demonstration, some of the locals start showing off. They jump into the river and swim close to where we are fishing; one of them explains to us helpfully that it's only dangerous to swim if you have a cut. They beckon us in, but there are no takers ...

After Christmas in Corumbá, from where our Pantanal safari was launched, Marcus heads west to Bolivia. This is where I leave him; but I have no plans of my own as yet, just a vague notion to travel south while the weather is still warm. I take a bus to Sao Paulo, then on a whim jump straight onto another bus to Rio. Based on an old recommendation, I decide to head there for the New Years Eve celebrations.

Although I am back to where I started, I feel my decision is vindicated when I see the massive party that's laid out in front of me on Copacabana beach to welcome in 1989. Amongst the throngs of revellers, transvestites and acrobats are two massive sound-stages and dozens of stalls selling fresh caipirinhas, that favourite Brazilian cocktail of cashaça and limes. I use them as pitstops as I cruise the beach front.

Later I bump into a few friends along the way, and we score some grass from a gang of street kids. They eye up my pockets surreptitiously, but I have come prepared for thieves; I have just enough money for the evening stored in a pouch sewn into the inside of my trousers. However, as the evening progresses and my inebriation increases, so my vigilance deteriorates in equal proportion. Each time now that I check my pockets, something new has gone missing - a lighter, a pack of cigarettes, some loose change, finally my wallet. By then though, I have rendered myself totally carefree, and find enough generosity amongst the locals to keep me going for the remainder of the night.

As the sun rises the next morning, I hang off the side of a bus that's heading back towards my hotel. A policeman stops the bus at a roadblock and frisks me. I smile at him knowingly - for there is absolutely nothing to be found ...

After a week in Rio, I finally head south. This route takes me through a relatively affluent part of South America, through southern Brazil and Uruguay to Argentina. The streets of the Uruguayan capital Montevideo are full of well preserved vintage American cars, something I am an avid fan of, but unfortunately it's the launderette that devotes most of my attention at this time. I have caught fleas from a seedy hotel in Curitiba, their small itchy bites appearing round my waist day and night, and in front of me now, spinning soapily, are all the clothes that I possess barring one pair of shorts. The next day, however, the fleas return, perhaps having rested comfortably in my hotel bed while I presumed I was drowning them in the washing machine. It's not until a night bus ride into Buenos Aires a few days later, that I sense them jump off me onto one particularly unkempt passenger sitting next to me. It is a huge relief.

Buenos Aires feels very much like a European city, complete with wide avenues, ornamental parks, government palaces and even its own version of Harrods. The Falklands war is still recent in memory, and the locals talk openly about it; most agree it was a waste of lives and criticise the governments on both sides, but they are genuinely surprised to hear that Thatcher is hated by the majority of British youth. I can't stay long in this town though; the exchange rate is prohibitively expensive, and I survive by eating in the 'all you can eat' buffet restaurants that scatter the city centre. It's in one of these that I run into an English girl, Penny, who I've met several times travelling the same route from Rio; she even shared my flea infestation from Curitiba, though it's unclear which one of us picked them up first. We are not overly compatible, but we are travelling in the same direction, so we decide to join forces as we head further south towards Chile.

The trip takes us by train to Bariloche, a town in the Andes that resembles an Austrian ski resort, complete with chalets, chocolate shops and St. Bernard dogs. There are rumours that the Nazis escaped to this area after the second world war, and I see enough Teutonic old men wandering the streets to arouse my own suspicions. Certainly there is no sense of being in Argentina at all.

From there we cross the Andes into Chile by bus and by boat, traversing the clear waters of some of the most beautiful mountain lakes I've ever seen. When we reach the south of Chile, we find the simple tranquility of small fishing towns full of weatherboard houses and weather-beaten fishermen, with rooms to rent in local's houses and seafood cooked freshly in the markets.

But it is the journey north from there that has me most excited. We have read in the papers of a recent volcanic eruption in Lonquimay, a small detour on the way to Santiago. After three bus rides, we hitch a ride up the mountain on the back of a pickup truck, both of us beginning to freeze from the increasing altitude; we pass through various checkpoints on the steep winding road until we eventually break through the clouds after dark. Coming to a halt barely a hundred yards from the eruption, it is an incredible sight. A firework display of epic proportions is played out in front of us, and the heat from the lava roasts our skin. But what will last most in the memory are the thunderous booms of the explosive rocks, which in the echo of the crater sound like massive steel warehouse doors being slammed shut over and over again. It is a humbling reminder of the power of nature ...

At first sight the capital Santiago is vast, noisy and polluted, with fleets of old buses belching out smoke as they criss-cross the city grid; but it soon proves to be another of those cities that is hard to leave.

Chile has gone through a ruthless dictatorship under Pinochet for many years and has only recently seen foreign visitors returning in numbers. After so many of the opposition went missing in the seventies, the population here have become hugely politicised and are keen to tell their story to the outside world. Everywhere we go we are invited into homes, for dinners or for parties, and their concern is as much about how their country is perceived to foreigners as it is about their long struggle against an oppressive regime.

I am able to relate more to these stories when on the second day I encounter tear gas and water cannon in the street. I run instinctively in the direction of the fleeing crowd, without really understanding why; I am later told that the police were breaking up illegal street traders. On another occasion, I witness a peaceful demonstration against the arrest of a cardinal which is broken up in similar fashion; a few days later, a bomb goes off near our hotel for which we never discover the cause. It all just seems to be part of the day to day existence here.

But despite the occasional violence, I spend over three weeks in Santiago, most of it filled with social endeavours. It is common for me to be walking back to the hotel from some party or other in the early hours of the morning, often jeered at by police at checkpoints, and indulging in a habit I've developed of tucking small banknotes into the socks of sleeping tramps. For some reason I am amused by that mystifying moment of discovery that will greet them the next morning.

And just before I head north from here, I too have my own pleasant surprise. Amongst the letters awaiting me at the Poste Restante is a typewritten letter from Kurt, this time more upbeat. Here is an excerpt:

A.D.A.T.W. (Alcohol and Drug Abuse Throughout the World) - Holland Corp.
To the honorable professor Sir Jon.
Hello, I'm sitting here typing with in my left hand a beer and in the right

hand a joint. Now this seems rather impossible to, allow me to say, normal people. But for a professor in alcohol and drug abuse it's just routine. Being completely bored most of the time, I borrowed this typewriter to do a bit of work concerning our studies about alcohol and drug abuse in Asia, Australia and the Eastblock. Its a big job: sorting out all the documents about drug rituals in S.E. Asia, the alcohol abuse of the average Australian (shocking results) and how to score champagne and vodka in Moscow (this on special request of Ronald Reagan). Beside all that I have 14 channels on my T.V. which I try to see all at the same time because there is nothing of any interest on it. Only BBC1 and 2 has some stuff of interest: snooker, darts and now the F.A. Cup, Oxford just lost to Manchester 4-0, too bad.

Ladst (godver de godverdomme fucking typewriter) I just try again: Last night I got a phone call from one of our students, Stacey, I'm sure you remember her, she was very talented, bright and very eager to learn. She told me she is a trainee yuppy now and is going to get married on the 13th May, how strange life can be indeed! A very talented girl with enormous possibilities for the future and then something like this happens. It's maybe a bit like the two of us, I mean did our parents ever expect that we would end up this high on the social ladder of life?????

I probably told you this shit before but my apologies for repeating things, I'm probably going to an island in the north of Holland in June, I heard from some people it's some kind of celebration thing with loads of freaks. Maybe I can spread the word a bit and find some lost souls to teach them some of our religion.

I'm about to finish this letter, I hope it will arrive in time and in the right spot. Let me know what's happening in this paradise of yours, take it easy on the booze, drugs and birds (only joking). For me its time for some relaxing smoke after a hard days work. Wish you all the best and please take good care of yourself,

Fellow professor, King and mate, Kurt x

It was good timing for me to get this correspondence, I had begun to miss the humour and camaraderie of someone like Kurt; and it turns out to be somewhat portentous. For I am soon to run into just that treasured thing. On a bus between Antofogasta and Calama, I find myself sat next to two strangers, Nick and Eran, a Kiwi and Israeli respectively. They have been travelling together since meeting on a kibbutz four long years ago. And we are soon to become not only friends, but also business partners ...

14. peru

As we reach the Atacama Desert with its backdrop of distant snowcapped mountains, there is a sense now that everyone is travelling in the same direction. Penny is still with me, but a loose group is forming around us that is growing larger by the day. They are all here to catch the weekly train to Bolivia, a popular route on the way to the ultimate destination of Machu Picchu in Peru; we are now officially on the Gringo Trail. The desert itself is beautiful, and we all pay a visit to the lunar valley in San Pedro at sundown, where a technicoloured landscape of alien rock formations is transformed by the moonlight. After that, we are ready for the train.

It sets off before lunch at crawling pace, climbing inexorably towards the Bolivian plateau which sits at around four thousand metres high. Although we leave the station wearing T-shirts, the rising altitude brings with it the cold, and by the end of our long ascent I have accumulated several layers inside a cocoon of blankets. Out of the window the first llamas appear, grazing amongst the loose stone walls which criss-cross the grassy plains. I am sitting with Nick and Eran now, trading tales from our travelling past, and after crossing into Bolivia the next day, I am suddenly compelled into making a choice. Penny walks into our carriage to tell me she is getting off at the next stop, travelling with another group to the silver mines of Potosi; Nick and Eran, however, are staying on to Oruro. It's an easy decision: I instinctively stay on the train; the prospect of good company supersedes any thoughts I have about seeing the sights.

Nick is a semi-professional photographer who has had his photographs and stories published in New Zealand travel magazines; he can be both intense and witty, but rarely anything in-between; proud of his half Maori descent, these origins are evident in his dark countenance and muscular build, and may also account for a hint of controlled aggression that lurks behind his piercing blue eyes. Eran on the other hand, is a kibbutz worker of Iranian descent and of much gentler and easy going disposition. The talk amongst us now is of what lies ahead, with little attention spared for the country through which we pass. We all have only one thing on our minds at this stage of our journey: to prepare for Peru ...

As sure as every good story of inspiration and triumph will travel, so the tales of trials and misfortune will often travel further. And every story we have heard coming out of Peru has involved robbery or theft of some description. Not one of the travellers we've met has avoided parting with at least one of their possessions, be it money, passport, camera or backpack. There have been no exceptions.

And so, having settled in to our hotel in Oruro, we go shopping. First we require sacks to cover our bags, thus preventing easy identification by thieves when in the luggage hold of a bus; then chicken wire, to line the aforementioned sacks and prevent thieves from cutting into the bags, whether it's resting on a luggage rack or carried on your back; and finally, for that most primitive line of defence, we have decided to arm ourselves with baseball bats.

We manage to purchase all of these items from just one hardware store, with pitchfork handles providing the raw material for the bats. These hardwood sticks we carefully carve and sand to our own personalised designs, all of them embarrassingly and inescapably phallic in nature. Finally we spray the wood with three coats of black paint for a professional finish, with the hopeful logic that this will somehow make them less likely to be confiscated. By the end of the process, our hotel room resembles a busy carpenters workshop filled with thick toxic fumes; fortunately the manager shows little concern.

My stick now fits perfectly inside a rolled up blanket strapped to the top of my sports bag, which when carried on my left shoulder allows me to draw my weapon like a sword from its sheath. I am pretty sure I could break an arm or a leg with a good swing of it. We are ready. And it feels like we are going to war.

Our next stop is La Paz. The introduction to the capital of Bolivia is not what you would expect. As we pass the sign that welcomes us to the city, there is only a flat dreary suburb laid out for miles in front of us, indicating the start of a rather uninspiring low-rise metropolis. But shortly afterwards comes a revelation. The bus reaches the top of a valley and there, laid out below like a miniature city at the bottom of a crater, is the high rise centre of La Paz. It seems strange now to be descending five hundred metres into what is nevertheless the highest capital in the world.

Since we have arrived in Bolivia we have been adjusting to the altitude in traditional style. The coca leaf is widely used by locals to combat the lethargy and headaches that are symptomatic of mild altitude sickness. It is chewed in the mouth with banana ash, an alkali which extracts the drug from the leaf, and the sensation is not unlike filling your mouth with bay leaves and charcoal, then trying to grind this sour and stony mix into a pulp. The difference here is that your lips and gums soon become reassuringly numb from the cocaine, useful perhaps if you have a toothache. But we quickly discard this unpleasant habit when we discover a far more appetising way of taking this medicine in the form of coca tea. We buy these leaves from the indigenous Indians, who sell their wares on street corners dressed in colourful robes and bowler hats, ironically a legacy of the Spanish occupation rather than their own historic culture. They seem to be a quiet presence here, rarely interacting with foreigners and generally occupying only the poorest positions in the community. It is a sad sight in that regard, but not dissimilar to the indigenous populations of many other continents.

We make only one more stop on our way to Peru, a pretty town on the shores of Lake Titicaca called Copacabana. Arriving at a busy time of year when an Easter festival is taking place, our bus is blocked by a procession, with the bizarre sight of an effigy of Jesus being carried in a glass coffin to the top of a candle lit hill overlooking the lake. The town is full of pilgrims, once again the indigenous Indians who no doubt inherited their Catholicism from Spain, and many have walked the hundred mile trek from La Paz for their penance. Our own penance, however, is soon forthcoming, as we are forced to visit every single one of its two dozen hotels before we can finally secure the last room in town.

The next day we cross the Peruvian border with suitable vigilance. As we disembark from our bus in Puno, the driver obligingly warns us to be careful with our bags. His comments mark the beginning of an education that will make us all learned doctors in the art of thievery, taught by a nation that has neither the moral concerns nor the limits of ingenuity to restrain them. We will come to believe that the conspiracy against the traveller does not only arise from a small criminal minority, but is also very much institutional. And it is not very long before we are taught our first lesson ...

The train from Puno to Cusco stops in Juliaca station once every evening. And every evening the same ritual can be observed: the lights of the train are switched off for two minutes, and a gang of thieves are allowed to scour the carriages, relieving travellers of as many bags as they can muster in the time. In the dark, they use both stealth and distraction to ply their trade, as bag after bag is thrown through the open windows and doors to accomplices on the platforms. But we have been warned. Our bags are either chained to the racks or clutched tightly in our arms. For some further down the carriage, however, there is a rude awakening. One of a group of three young Englishmen has lost his knapsack, containing a camera and eight rolls of exposed film - memories of his last two months of travel. They are the same group that Nick and I had argued with in our hotel the night before; they were sympathetic to the thieves, citing their poverty as justifiable cause; we, however, maintained that the gangs were not poor but rich, as witnessed by the expensive clothes and watches they wear. As a result, we feel little sympathy towards them now; Nick delivers the coup de grâce by congratulating them on their charitable contribution ...

As we set off on the short walk from Cusco station to our intended hotel, we put our preparation into practice; with sticks at the ready, we eyeball the many well-healed thieves who hang out on the street corners along the way, as if to dare them to accost us. They do not. They smile in recognition and quickly divert their attention elsewhere. And with that first important task successfully accomplished, we can settle into the hotel and relax ...

Cusco is a beautiful city, with its Spanish style terracotta tiled roofs and whitewashed walls built on the earthquake-proof foundations of the Incas. The crazy-pave style Inca stones are cut so intricately that their straight edges fit together without the need for mortar, and they are still visible on many of the historical buildings around town. We stay in a hotel just off the Plaza de Armas, a pleasant garden square with scenic views of the surrounding hills and a focal point of the city. It's here that I run into Penny again, and we swap stories; she has just met three girls who were robbed at the market here - they had been kicked and punched as the locals stood around watching and laughing. I, in turn, recount the story of a traveller I met in Puno who discovered that his dollar bills had been replaced with fakes inside the hotel safe; the management had denied any involvement, and the police had refused to help. So common are these tales that they frequently dominate the conversation.

After a few days, I set off for Machu Picchu with Nick and Eran. First we take the bus to Urubamba, and then on to Ollantaytambo where we stop to see the lesser known Inca ruins there and stay for the night. It's a beautiful trip by itself, but it also allows us to take the local train to Machu Picchu further up the line and avoid paying in dollars for the expensive tourist train from Cusco. We board the crowded carriage with a bottle of pisco to accompany us, and spend the two hour journey standing up, taking intermittent swigs of the colourless brandy from a brown paper bag. In retrospect, it was not a wise thing to do; the combination of spirits and altitude can be a lethal cocktail. A little the worse for wear, we disembark at Aguas Calientes where we find a cheap hotel to stay only a few kilometres from the ruins.

The scene is now set for a pivotal moment involving a small electronic device that in many ways resembles an electric shaver. Nick has come to Peru prepared not only with his own customised baseball bat, but also with something far handier - a stun gun. Purchased from one of the ubiquitous Korean traders in Paraguay, it can deliver two hundred thousand volts in a couple of seconds, enough to drop a fully grown man. And as we sit drinking pisco into the night at one of the cafes, Nick decides that this is an appropriate time to test out his new toy; first on a stray dog which has approached us looking for food and then, when I protest against this cruelty, on my very own outstretched leg.

To understand what follows we must envision an imaginary switch inside my head that, though normally pointed to 'merry', has now flipped over to 'mad'; it is probably true to say that, when inebriated to this extent, those two divergent settings are the only ones available to me. I jump on Nick. We roll on the floor, tables and chairs are overturned and, not without a struggle, we are separated by Eran and a few bemused bystanders.

Soon afterwards, as I am collecting the room key at the hotel reception to head mercifully for my bed, I am approached by three plain clothed police flashing their badges; they immediately demand that I hand over the bottle of pisco still clasped firmly in my right hand. As any drunk will testify, this is a request that is hard to grant in any circumstance; and whether it is for this blunt refusal or for the earlier more serious altercation, I am nevertheless led away to the police station.

This short journey takes much longer than expected. As we start to head down the railway tracks into the murky darkness, I am overcome by a growing realisation that the police may not be what they seem; they could, after all, be thieves carrying false IDs. I try to break away from them but am dragged literally kicking and screaming up the tracks, with hands clinging tight to the sleepers until forcibly removed. When we finally arrive at a shack at the end of the tracks, I am relieved to see that Nick and Eran are there waiting for me. Now, with Eran as the mediator, we insist that Nick and I are friends, that there has been a misunderstanding, and that we are now calm enough to go home quietly. The police seem almost convinced ... until in comical fashion, after a wrong word spoken under the breath, Nick and I break out into a fight once more ...

I spend the night on the dirt floor of a small cell behind floor-to-ceiling bars, and awake in the early hours, flea bitten and disorientated, with no knowledge of where I am. I scream out in panic, and Nick appears on the other side of the bars like a vision, reminding me painfully of what happened the night before. It becomes a long traumatic night for me, until at six in the morning we are finally released in the morning light; our passports, however, are inauspiciously retained by the police ...

We make the hard climb up to Machu Picchu with the rising sun, and are rewarded with an almost deserted site when we arrive; it's not until about ten in the morning that the tourist buses arrive, ferrying the first passengers from the Cusco train. It is understandable why these ruins are so highly regarded; although there are other well preserved Inca settlements in Peru, this one has an incomparable setting, sitting on the saddle of a twin peaked mountain rising fifteen hundred meters above the canyon below. Once inhabited by a commune of five hundred Incas in the fifteenth century, some of the houses have been carefully reconstructed to their original design complete with timbers and thatched roofs. In the middle of the day I sleep soundly inside one of the grassy ruins while the hustle and bustle of the midday visitors carries on around me. In the evening the place falls silent again, and after a last tranquil meditation in this beautiful setting, we head back to the town.

Returning to the police station, Nick and I now face the consequences of our transgressions. As our two passports sit ominously on the desk in front of us, the events of the previous evening are retold in detail by both parties.

This from the policemen's side with expressions of hurt pride: there was kicking and punching, even bruising to the body; what will the chief of police say when he hears about this? No, there is only one thing for it - they will have to deport us from Peru. A red stamp is procured and held menacingly over our passports ...

Then quickly from our side in broken Spanish: we were taken by surprise by the strength of the pisco; they wore no uniforms, they could have been thieves. A wholehearted apology is offered for this misunderstanding; how can we possibly make amends?

A thoughtful silence ensues.

"Maybe we can help each other," the most senior one hints, with the stamp hovering close to the page of my passport.

"What kind of help do you need?" I ask, now fearful of the figure he has in mind. Earlier they had been admiring Nick's camera equipment, asking the price of each item one by one.

"Maybe our station needs a new coat of paint," another suggests. My mind spins fast in calculation.

"Would twenty dollars cover it?" I suggest tentatively.

A pause.

"Amigos!" they cry, and with hands held out for rigorous shaking we have ourselves a deal. Nick and I give each other a look of undisguised relief.

Still in awe of the camera equipment, they invite us back the following day to take a professional photograph of them. Eran takes charge of the camera, as Nick and I stand side by side with two of the policemen posing manfully with their Kalashnikovs. For the second photo, however, we are handed their guns to hold. Together we look like a ragbag gang of revolutionaries, and for something that has cost us ten dollars each, we are tempted to think it was worth it just for that one memorable photograph.

There was no bad feeling between Nick and I after that encounter, just an acknowledgement of each other's darker side. And as the three of us head back to Cusco and from there onwards to the coast, we unite against a common enemy once more: the gangs of Peruvian thieves.

The walk back to the station in Cusco is not without event: with little warning, Eran has his watch snatched off his wrist by a teenage boy creeping up from behind. There is nothing we can do; with packs on our back we cannot give chase, and the thief stands cockily just ten yards away admiring his new acquisition. In Juliaca station the lights go out on schedule, and the familiar shouts can be heard as bags are removed from the carriages. Then, as we pass through the white walled town of Arequipa, we hear another tale of ingenuity. Thieves at the bus station have posed as staff behind an empty counter, insisting that a traveller checks in his backpack before the journey; the real bus company turns up later, claiming no knowledge of the bag. In the same town, I myself have a close call with a conman. A seemingly helpful man on the street offers a good rate on my travellers cheques and takes me to an office where I can change them; but when asked to sit in a waiting area so that he can take the cheque to his friend, I quickly walk away. It's an obvious con; if I give him the cheque, he will no doubt disappear out of a door at the back.

Our next stop is Nazca, famous for its giant figures drawn in the desert by an ancient civilisation. Although they can be seen most clearly from the air, we decide that the flights are not worth the cost, perhaps even a little too dangerous; instead, we blow our budget on a rundown hotel with a rare luxury - a swimming pool - taking the opportunity while we can for some relaxation off the road. We satisfy our curiosity for the Nazca lines by viewing them from close up and from the nearby hills, spending the rest of our stay by the pool. And after a few days of this well deserved R&R, we resume our journey to the capital ...

Lima welcomes us in its own inimitable way. As we approach the bus station, two armed guards open a massive pair of security doors to let our bus in, keeping a large crowd at bay outside. After disembarking, we prepare ourselves to face the throng outside the gates; arms wrapped tightly around our possessions, we quickly run the gauntlet and jump into the first available taxi. On our short journey through the city, the streets that we pass through look dirty and decayed, with the only real respite an impressive colonial square glimpsed just before we arrive at our hotel.

And so, regarding our continuing education, we have now reached the very pinnacle of learning. For this is not only the political and financial capital of Peru, but also very much its capital of petty crime, the tales of which are exchanged regularly between travellers like discussing the weather. As we settle in to our new surroundings at the Hotel España, we are warned of the latest con that is starting to become prevalent in the city: it starts innocently enough, with a boy stopping you in the street to ask for directions; if you make the mistake of engaging in conversation, you are approached by two plain-clothed policemen who search the boy and find a bag of cocaine. You are then arrested for attempting to buy drugs, and driven to a quiet street where you are extorted out of as much cash as possible; to deter any resistance, a gun rests menacingly on the dashboard. The American who tells me this story has lost three hundred dollars. But like all cons of this nature, the power is removed if you know the story in advance; all you need to do is simply walk away ...

And there is something in the heat of this crime wave that the three of us are beginning to take advantage of: we are scouring the markets for cut price cameras. Nick, because he is an aficionado and wants to enlarge his collection of lenses and bodies, Eran and I, because we want to step up to a professional camera for a good price. At this time in Peru, cameras are the most regularly stolen item, often snatched during the very act of taking a picture; those in the know use a metal strap to prevent it from being cut. The stolen cameras end up in the markets at rock bottom prices, and it becomes something of an obsession with us, as we scour the stalls making deals, swapping one body or lens for another.

And with this day to day business, we also discover girls. Nick has decided to continue a relationship with a Peruvian girl he met during our stay in Arequipa, while Eran has found a girlfriend amongst a group that regularly join our table at the local restaurant. Then, just as I am buying a bus ticket to head north towards Ecuador, a similar thing happens to me. Two girls follow me from the bus station back to the hotel, and I invite them to the bar next door for a drink; it soon transpires that one of them, Carmela, a pretty mestizo girl in her early twenties, has taken a shine to me. It doesn't take me long to decide to miss the bus and stay in Lima a little while longer.

It is easy to see in retrospect how on such small twists of fate rest a whole raft of consequences. For now that the three of us are ensconced in the city, this time with girlfriends in tow, we are in contemplative mood. With funds running low, we have been debating whether we could sell the cheap camera equipment from the market as a way of making money; the profits, however, would be small, and the morals distinctly dubious. It seems out of the question.

But it is in this frame of mind that we receive the news of a fortuitous meeting. Eran has run into an Israeli couple in the street who have been touring the continent in a VW Kombi van; they had bought the van in Brazil for two thousand dollars, and have just sold it in Lima for an astonishing five and a half thousand dollars. With a profit margin so high, and an overland adventure thrown in for good measure, this is an opportunity that will prove impossible to ignore ...

15. the business

It turns out that there are a number of reasons for the disparity in the cost of a Kombi van between Peru and Brazil. Primarily there is a very high import tax on cars in Peru, equal to the value of the car, and in consequence the heavy demand for cheaper second hand cars keeps those prices high as well. The Kombi in particular retains its value, as it's widely used throughout Lima as a shared taxi business and is therefore highly desired by budding entrepreneurs. Then, for foreigners such as ourselves, there are two convenient loopholes in the law. Unlike Peruvian nationals, we are allowed to bring a car into Peru without paying import tax, and although that still doesn't allow us to sell the car tax free, this is where the second loophole comes into play. A simple visit to a lawyer can set this up: the buyer loans a sum of money, the purchase price, to the seller using the car as collateral; the seller defaults on the loan and forfeits the car in due process; the buyer can then take legal possession of the car. In this scenario, which involves writing up a few documents and going before a judge, no tax is payable.

And so for us, a business is born. If we can do one run successfully, then we should be able to do more, and each run could buy us three to six months of extra travelling. The quickest route back to Brazil by road is four thousand miles through Chile and Argentina, crossing the Andes at Mendoza; we take consecutive buses day and night, and cover the distance in less than a week. We have chosen Curitiba as the city to buy our Kombis - it's the nearest big commercial centre in Brazil - though naturally we avoid the hotel that gave me those pesky fleas some five months earlier. And despite the bureaucracy that requires documents to be stamped at five different offices around town, we manage to buy our Kombis in less than two weeks; Nick and Eran share the cost of a pristine white two thousand dollar model, whilst mine is older and cheaper at twelve hundred dollars, in a tired looking beige colour to reflect its somewhat inferior status. There are a few more frustrating days to wait while the ownership is transferred to our names, but when it's done we are more than ready. All that lies ahead of us now is that four thousand miles of road ...

I can smell burning, the first signs of an impending disaster. It's only twenty minutes since we set off in our convoy of two at dusk, and now I can see smoke rising from the engine at the back. I signal to Nick to stop, and we open up the boot and look inside. The solenoid is billowing smoke, close to starting a fire. It dies down after a while with the engine switched off, and we decide to drive on to find a replacement part. But Nick is restless. After waiting for me to install a rusty looking unit found in the back of a garage workshop further up the road, he loses patience with the convoy and overtakes me, gesticulating wildly. He pulls away from me easily as my engine struggles to keep up, and after his lights have disappeared into the distance I am hit by a sudden sinking feeling: I can smell burning again. I have travelled barely ten miles since the replacement.

Fortunately Nick and I have arranged to meet at a hotel in Foz do Iguaçu in the event of losing each other, and I am still hopeful I can catch them up. But what follows is a painfully slow stop-start journey, limping up the road five miles at a time with twenty minute breaks for the burning solenoid to cool. There are no more garages to be found on this stretch of road - I am far into the countryside now - and as the burning becomes worse, I pull up for the night on a farm track somewhere in the middle of this wilderness. For several minutes there is a flicker of flames on the solenoid threatening to spread elsewhere in the engine, and I watch intently as the fate of my venture hangs in the balance. The flames wither and die. Reprieved, but still distraught, I wallow in my misfortune with the wailing sounds of a Smiths tape playing loudly on my radio-cassette, until finally falling asleep exhausted on a back bench. Like the night that I was stranded in Geneva, this feels like defeat.

The next day, however, I awake with renewed energy. The early morning somehow casts a new light and optimism on the situation. With thoughts of turning back cast aside, I set off in search of the next big town. I am able to drive much further after the engine has cooled overnight, and I reach it with only three cooling stops. This time a brand new, shiny solenoid is installed by a mechanic and I set off once again, hurrying to make my rendezvous with Nick and Eran, still three hundred miles away. But I soon discover that the problem with my engine is not the solenoid itself, when ten miles up the road I come to another smoky halt. Now a third mechanic looks at my engine and its freshly burnt replacement part; I have no reason to trust this one any more than the previous two, but after conjuring up yet another rusty solenoid, he calmly swaps the wires going to the positive and negative terminals and sends me on my way. After twenty smoke free miles, I breathe a sigh of relief. I am finally on my way.

And now in hindsight, as I drive relentlessly towards my destination without stopping, I am able to trace back the source of this misfortune. Prior to the trip, I took my Kombi to be checked over by a mechanic in Curitiba; he must have switched the wires by accident. That precautionary measure has now cost me three solenoids and ten hours of breakdowns. And there is a further consequence, a final blow. When I reach Foz do Iguaçu as night is drawing in, I check into the hotel and ask for Nick and Eran. They are not there. But they have, thoughtfully, left me a message at the reception:

'Sorry, we couldn't wait any longer. If you made it this far, good luck and see you in Lima! Nick and Eran.'

The next morning I set off for Argentina, resigned to making this long journey on my own. They have two drivers working shifts with a day's head start, and it will be almost impossible to catch them up. I decide, therefore, to take my time and go at my own pace.

Argentina is a vast country with a complex web of roads, and I navigate by connecting the dots on a rudimentary map from an old guidebook; sometimes the towns that I've picked out for my route disappear from signposts, and I am lost for hours, retracing my steps. I drive day and night, and when the cold sets in after dark, I lay blankets over my legs like an old man, shivering and cursing the fact that no heaters were ever installed in these Brazilian Kombis. On one such evening, I am stopped by police. Apparently I have a defective light, but with a few well aimed kicks of my boot it soon flickers back into action. They immediately change tack and ask me to produce a warning triangle, something they know I won't have; in fact it is unlikely that any car on the Argentinian roads possesses one of these, but on threat of escorting me to the police station I negotiate a ten dollar 'fine' instead. The next day, I am wondering how I will avoid all these extra costs, when a solution presents itself. I pick up a group of hitchhikers along the way and one of them turns out to be a policeman; we sail through the next few police checkpoints with a wave of his hand, and I now resolve to pick up everyone I possibly can at the roadside.

After four long days of driving through Argentina sleeping in the back of the van, I am able to treat myself to a hotel bed in Mendoza. The Argentinian currency has collapsed since I was last travelling through, and everything is now half the price it was; I struggled to survive here before, staying in hostels and eating cheap buffet meals, but now I can check into a three star hotel and order steak for dinner. It's a rare moment of luxury, and the hot shower and warm duvet are like an oasis in the desert. It occurs to me how different my experience of Argentina would have been if my timing had been better.

The following morning I set off early to cross the Andes. The pass rises to over three thousand metres, and the climb is slow in my old and pedestrian Kombi. I stop periodically to adjust the carburettor which needs more air as the altitude increases; I am no mechanic, but it's easy enough to hear the engine improve when turning the appropriate screw. Halfway up this ponderous ascent, I spot two hitchhikers at the side of the road and pull over without a moment's hesitation; it's two girls, Alejandra and Lidia, and they turn out to be excellent company. Both from Cordoba and in their late twenties, they are taking time out to visit friends in Santiago.

We approach the capital of Chile in good spirits, and although my intention is to drop them off in the outskirts and head up north, I miss my turning and find myself in heavy rush hour traffic headed for the centre. Unsettled by the speed and chaos of the highway, I am suddenly confronted by a stationary car. With little time to break, I swerve to avoid it; but the turning circle of the Kombi is woeful, and it clips the left tail of the car before coming to a shuddering halt. I am in shock.

I pull over to the side of the road to find that my front right wing has caved in, in similar fashion to the car's rear left wing; and the three male occupants of that car are now very angry. Immediately they demand money, and although my Spanish is now passable, I instinctively feign misunderstanding. Instead, with the girls acting as translators for me, I suggest we call the police.

"They don't want the police, they have no insurance," Alejandra tells me.

"How much are they asking for?"

"They are crazy, they want five hundred dollars."

"No way," I say. "Their whole car isn't worth that, it's a wreck."

I explain that I don't have that kind of money; in fact I don't have much cash on me at all, certainly not enough to appease them. There is an uneasy stalemate for several minutes, and one of them tears a wing mirror off my Kombi in vengeful frustration. Then Alejandra says to me quickly:

"We must go. I heard them talking. One of them has gone off to get more friends, they want to smash your Kombi."

I need no more invitation. We drive off without a word, fleeing the scene as fast as possible. I feel responsible for the accident, but helpless nevertheless.

That night I rest up with one of their Chilean friends in Santiago. We sleep the three of us huddled in a spare double bed, and the friend buys us beer to soothe our nerves. He turns out to be a lawyer and suggests I report the incident to the police in case they have done the same. I do this the following morning, then decide to have an extra night of recuperation with this typical Chilean hospitality. Over dinner, Alejandra and Lidia have a proposal for me.

"We'd like to come with you to Peru. It's always been our dream to go to Cusco, and it seems to be fate that you are driving that way."

"Of course you can come," I say.

"But there's a problem. We don't have any money. Nothing at all..." There's a pause. "But we are very cheap to feed, and we will help any way we can. We are good at getting favours because we are girls."

I thought about this for a while. I was tight on money too, I didn't want to run out before I could sell the Kombi. But I'd already seen how helpful they could be, and their company would make my trip that much more enjoyable. In the end it was an easy decision.

The Pan-American highway that runs north to Peru through Chile is long and empty, hugging the Pacific ocean at times with hundreds of miles of empty beaches. But our journey is kept interesting by picking up every hitchhiker we see. Often the benches in the back are full, with new passengers making introductions to old as they jump in and out; at one time the van is full of children who belong to a school choir, and they regale us loudly with their long repertoire of songs. Meanwhile, Alejandra and Lidia do not disappoint on their promises. We are often bought lunch by the locals in roadside cafes, mostly through their charm, but also from a strong tradition of hospitality amongst the Chileans. One truck driver explains to me:

"When you are in my house, I offer you food. When I am in your house, you offer me. But here you are in my house, Chile."

We reach Antofogasta on the third day with some interesting news awaiting us. I spot a Volkswagen garage with a few Kombis on jacks and ask them if they've seen a white one driven by two foreigners recently. It turns out that they have; Nick and Eran have just left town. They were here for three days of repairs after the transmission fell out a few hundred miles down the road. I can't help but indulge myself in a joyous moment of schadenfreude at hearing this. Only one day behind them, I feel like a celebration is in order, and soon enough I get another excuse.

Alejandra has been talking about how she is hungry for 'vitaminas', but 'not the kind you get in food'. With a suitably flirtatious look on her face, I think I have understood this as sexual innuendo, but am unsure until later that evening when Lidia takes me aside and explains:

"Alejandra would like to have sex with you. But she likes a drink to get her in the mood."

At the next stop I buy two bottles of wine.

Two more days driving and we arrive at the Peruvian border. For me it's a nervous encounter - I need to get through without any financial penalties on my Kombi. After some delay, a customs officer sat behind a large paper-strewn desk tells me I have to give him fifty dollars to get my papers stamped; I ask what the fifty dollars is for. There is no attempt at subterfuge:

"For me," he replies matter-of-factly.

Reluctant to pay another bribe, I relay this to Alejandra, who tells me to wait in the car. After five minutes, she comes out of the official's hut, arm in arm with Lidia. She holds up the stamped papers to me and breaks into a grin.

"What did you say to him?"

"I told him we hadn't eaten for two days, and then we both burst into tears."

Lidia and Alejandra can now officially say they have paid their way for this trip.

Peru of course is well known to me now, and I am no longer picking up hitchhikers. Soon after the border we are climbing towards Arequipa through a desert landscape. The hill is steep, and the Kombi is struggling to make 10 mph in second gear. I spot a man in the distance standing on a bluff next to the side of the road - it's an odd sight, there are no signs of civilisation as far as the eye can see, and he stares down the road at us with arms tucked casually behind his back. As we approach him, his eyes lock into mine for several beats, his raised position allowing him a dominant view into our cabin. He makes no movement at all apart from a slow turn of the head as he tracks us, his face locked into a faint smile. All three of us feel the tension. As soon as we're past, I look in the mirror and see that behind his back he is holding a gun. I look at Alejandra, my head spinning with what-ifs: would he have pulled the gun on me if I'd been alone? Was the gun even loaded? I will never know. Perhaps, like me, he suspects I would have called his bluff and kept on driving up the hill ...

I drop the girls in Arequipa and give them enough money for bus tickets to Cusco - it's as much as I can spare. The final leg to Lima I will have to do on my own, on one of the most dangerous roads in South America. The worst part runs for a hundred and twenty miles along the coast shortly after Arequipa, where it twists and turns along a mountainous precipice that falls steeply into the sea on one side. It is heavily potholed and prone to rockfalls for which I have been warned to be particularly wary, as they can sometimes be staged by bandits. But far more dangerous is the traffic. This stretch is busy with trucks and buses driving recklessly around corners trying to keep to their schedules, often through a heavy mist that descends regularly along these shores. There have been many accidents reported in recent months, with buses careering off the cliffs; TEPSA, the biggest bus company in Peru, has lost two in a week. I had already made this journey twice myself, the most recent a hair-raising ride at night through the fog, with locals weeping and crossing themselves as our bus hurtled blindly around the bends.

Correspondingly, I negotiate this road with great care and respect. I am fortunate in one regard; I am heading north, and the ocean drop is on the opposite side. The journey soon becomes a marathon of concentration, where every corner hides one obstacle or another, and a constant zigzagging is required to avoid damaging the Kombi in one of those giant potholes. I finish the stretch in ten hours of painfully slow driving, but the relief is palpable: ahead of me now lies only two more days of driving, along a much easier road. Soon I will be in Lima ...

It wouldn't be much of an exaggeration to say that for the last sixteen days I had been imagining the look on Nick's face when I finally arrived in Lima. And as I walk through the door of the Hotel España, bumping into him on the way out, it's far better than I expected; something more than surprise - it's shock.

"I never thought you'd make it ..." he says incredulously. His eyes betray his own weariness from the journey he completed only two days earlier - the costly repairs in Chile must have taken its toll.

"Eran thought you would, but I didn't believe him," he continues. "Looks like I owe him ten bucks." There is almost disappointment in his tone, but it's not enough to dent my high spirits; my sense of accomplishment is all that more to have defied his expectations.

After a brief update on our respective journeys, we settle down to the business in hand: how to sell our Kombis. This being Peru, Nick directs me to a guarded car park where his own Kombi is kept a few streets away. It's a costly but necessary expense, as everything from windscreen wipers to wheel hubs are removed if you park in the street. And Nick has already found a lead through the nightwatchman who works there; apparently one of the customers is interested in Nick's Kombi and would like to see mine as well. After a quick phone call, a rendezvous is set for the next day.

Hector turns out to be a sincere and charming man. He owns his own garage and thinks he can sell my Kombi to his passing trade. He is less interested in Nick's Kombi, however, as the asking price for that one is too high - five and a half thousand dollars compared to four thousand for mine. We make a deal whereby eight hundred dollars is paid to me as deposit, returnable if he doesn't sell within three weeks; during this period, my Kombi will sit outside his garage on display. It is a huge leap of faith for me, but somehow I trust this man. It helps that he tells me stories of how fellow Peruvians, sometimes friends and colleagues, have stolen from him in the past; it seems that foreigners are not the only target here, just perhaps the easiest one.

Nevertheless, the day after we make the deal, the doubts set in. Hector has given me eight one hundred dollar bills. And at this time in Lima, rumours abound that some very good counterfeit hundreds from Columbia are in circulation; the street traders will only deal with fifties or twenties now. I know the checks: if you can feel the embossed cloak of the president and the embossed writing at the borders, it is likely to be real. But on examination of the eight specimens in my possession, the white framing is uneven and differs appreciably between the bills; it seems too untidy to be the product of the U.S. mint. The next day I confront Hector with this concern, and he quickly assures me they have been sourced from a bank. But as convincing as he is, the anxiety still remains ...

Life soon settles back into a rhythm. We are reunited with our girlfriends, and our social lives resume. I am invited to Carmela's twenty-third birthday party which I dutifully attend; but being my first visit to her home, I am totally unprepared for what awaits me. Chairs line the walls of the living room, and seated on them awkwardly but politely are about a dozen of her friends, all female, and all of them drinking orange squash. Throughout the evening I am paraded like the prize in a fairytale kingdom-wide search for a prince. The event only reinforces the realisation that I'm dating someone who still lives the life a protected young teenager. It's a cultural difference that's particularly hard to overcome, but the naivety has its charm, and I persevere nonetheless.

And when we are out together, we are often reminded of the dangerous city we inhabit. Leaving the cinema one afternoon after a matinee screening, I am attacked by a man reaching deep into my pockets for anything he can find. He kicks Carmela viciously as we both try to fight him off, but it's a struggle to pull his strong arms out of my pockets. He walks away calmly, examining the packet of cigarettes and biro that he's managed to procure, then turns to me and throws the pen on the ground in disgust; clearly such an item is beneath his contempt. Yet despite the daylight and the hundreds of onlookers, no one intervenes.

And it's not just the criminal element who seem out to get us. Late one night we are arrested by police on suspicion of prostitution, the clear evidence being that she looks local and I do not. It's only after half an hour of interrogation that we manage to extricate ourselves. It doesn't help that Carmela has forgotten my middle name, and I her address, but eventually we manage to convince them that our relationship is more than just a few hours old.

Meanwhile, time is moving relentlessly onwards, and there is a growing tension developing between Nick and I. The Kombis remain unsold, and we are all running out of cash - Nick and Eran far quicker than I am. In the third week, he confronts me with this problem:

"Let's break into one of those hundreds," he suggests.

But for me this is not an option. Hector could demand his deposit back at any moment, and I can't take that risk. I suggest instead that he sells one of the many camera lenses he has acquired since being in Peru. It doesn't go down well. If there was a rift there before, it has now opened up a little wider.

The following week, Hector finds a buyer for my Kombi. It's a woman who wants to use it for a school run, and she negotiates me down to three and a half thousand, after Hector's commission is taken out. When I finally get the money, it's all paid in twenty dollar bills, a wedge of notes almost an inch thick, with the eight hundred returned to Hector intact and unchallenged; but unfortunately it comes too late to prevent Nick from selling one of his precious lenses. A few days later, Nick and Eran are forced into accepting a low offer of four thousand for their Kombi. We are all immensely relieved. But there is no talk whatsoever of doing another run ...

On the day that Nick leaves town with his girlfriend to visit her parents in Arequipa, there is a festival blocking all the roads around the Hotel España and most of central Lima. It means I have to jog through the streets, dodging parades of musicians and stick twirlers, as I hurry anxiously towards the TEPSA bus station. Earlier, I had noticed something odd in their behaviour as they vacated the room we share at the hotel. I followed a hunch and counted my money; it was three hundred dollars short. In that moment I had known there were only two possible thieves, and both were still in Lima, waiting for a bus.

Sure enough, they are still sitting in the waiting room when I arrive panting from my fifteen minute run. I relate my recent discovery to them in a voice raised for everyone to hear.

"I want my money back," I insist calmly.

"What makes you think we've got it? It could have been the cleaner," Nick says.

"The cleaner wouldn't skim, she'd take it all and disappear. You both knew the hiding place. One of you stole it. Just be big enough to admit it."

Nick is clearly in conflict from my accusation. My sense is that his girlfriend is the instigator, and he regrets it; she and I don't get on very well. I've speculated during my jog that the three hundred might seem like a recoupment to him for the lesser profit he made on his Kombi; it is, coincidentally, the right sum to even things up.

"Look mate, I didn't take anything, you have to believe me."

He is passive, deflated even, and I can sense his guilt. But after a while, it is clear there will be no confession forthcoming. I leave the scene equally deflated. There have been no winners.

Soon after, Hector asks me to do another run; he would provide me with a detailed spec to buy the most profitable model of Kombi, and line up a buyer beforehand. It was what Nick, Eran and I had originally set out to do. But I turn him down. The fun for me is in the company I keep; to do it alone seems pointless.

And neither is Carmela a reason to stay anymore. The struggle to close that culture gap has continued for far too long, and I will leave her just as I found her: sweet, charming, beautiful, and still very much a virgin. So instead of continuing the business, I decide to head north from Peru and cross the border to Ecuador. There my journey can start afresh, and I will be on my own once again.

But before I go, there is an evening out organised by Hector to celebrate the sale of my Kombi. He and his girlfriend have invited Carmela and I to a summer fair which is running for a week long festival. It's a vast and crowded fairground, and he lends me his watch so that we can meet up later in the evening for dinner. When the time comes though, my wrist is empty; a quick bump in the crowd is all that was necessary for the watch to disappear. I break it to him gently. I am not sure of the protocol in this situation; is the liability mine or his? Despite nearly four months in this esteemed seat of learning, it seems that Peru will forever confound me.

the sword

What is there to say about this petty band of car runners, this gang of stab-in-the-back smugglers armed to the teeth with baseball bats?

By itself the account is crystalline in clarity, a direct confession, open-and-shut: a flagrant abuse of the law of taxation, wilfully perpetrated in shameful complicity. The prosecution need say no more ...

And where, if at all, should our sympathies lie in this sorry tale of deceit and betrayal? Is this not a tale as old as the hills, where those that live by the sword should surely expect to die by the sword?

Perhaps. But can it be said with hand on heart that this was indeed an immoral pursuit, a crime even? Where is the law transgressed? Where is the victim? The opposite may in fact be true; bear witness to the happy beneficiaries of such clandestine transactions - the hard working poor of Peru.

Yet how can we defend the absurd pugnacity of these two unruly protagonists? What brings a man to fight a friend that should unite to fight the enemy? A struggle for dominance? A vent of frustration?

I contend there may be darker, more primal forces at work here.
For in a place that has lost all reasonable containment of its criminal element, is it not a reaction normal to most to defend oneself, to be vigilant, to retaliate even? Does not the aggression of a society encourage in its subjects a similar return to primitive instinct?

For if you are seen only as meat to the hyenas, far better to stand tall and fight, than tamely submit to the kill ...

16. danger

Otto is playing outside when they come to visit. There are four of them, and each has an identification card held high for me to inspect.

"CID," says one.

It has no meaning to me other than how they appear - police who are casually dressed. Less like undercover, more like this is their day off.

"We have a tip-off. We will have to search your room."

My thoughts turn instantly to the landlord; maybe he smelt the grass I occasionally smoke in the room. Right now he is nowhere to be seen.

Jamila and I sit on the bed as two of them go to work on the room, and the other two stand awkwardly by. I have chained up the bedside table, where my money and passport reside, and shortly I am asked to unlock the padlock.

"They are looking for cash," Jamila whispers to me, translating their Swahili for me. "They think you are hiding a large sum somewhere."

Although this is something of a relief, I can see the second policeman moving perilously close to my stash in the wardrobe; the green of the grass is in plain sight from my position, nesting on an old piece of newspaper on the third shelf down. He is rifling through the top shelf now, soon to switch to the second.

My head is in overload, scrambling for a way out. They are looking for undeclared cash intended for the black market, which they can legally confiscate. The first policeman goes through my travellers cheques one by one, checking against my currency declaration form; it's a slow process, but I know that the paperwork is in order apart from a twenty pound note left undeclared as an emergency fund.

Meanwhile the second policeman has finished checking the second shelf and is about to switch to the third; he is about to strike gold unexpectedly - drug possession here carries the threat of prison and would likely extract the maximum bribe, all my money.

Suddenly I recognise this situation - police, robbers, riding close to a windfall - I've seen this all before. And the memories of those incidents in

South America are whispering to me a way out. I now know what I must do ...

Yishai is a dishevelled looking Israeli of half Iraqi descent, tall and unshaven with curly black hair. He is an unlikely companion for me; different in background and culture, yes, but more practically he doesn't speak a word of English. Yet as we sit across the communal dining table of a farm in the Ecuador mountains, we both quickly realise that we are the only travellers here that haven't arrived in a couple or a group. And from that small seed, a slow and unlikely dialogue of badly broken Spanish breaks out between us.

We are in Vilcabamba, a small town with apparently magical powers of longevity; it has been written up recently in the press as possessing more centenarians per capita than anywhere else in the world. Yet despite its reputation, there are very few old people to be seen; perhaps they are hidden indoors, or perhaps ironically they have all recently passed away. Nevertheless, amongst travellers, this place is famous for something far more tangible - the San Pedro cactus. A hallucinogenic containing mescaline, the plant grows wild in these parts and is harvested and distilled by an American who took up residence here many years ago.

The subject of the stilted conversation between Yishai and I is precisely this, and we make a plan to take the cactus together the following day, along with most of the farm's guests. First though, a visit is required to the American. We locate his dwelling down a small dirt road, following directions from the farm's owners, and knock gingerly on the door of a decrepit looking shack. A distant shout beckons us in. The room we enter is small and cluttered, with shelves full of dusty bottles of all descriptions, like an alchemist's secret den. The American appears at the back door.

"We heard you might be brewing up some cactus," I ask cautiously.

"You guys are in luck. I have a batch cooking right now," he replies in a businesslike manner. "Follow me, I'll show you."

He looks exactly how I imagined him: bearded and ponytailed with John Lennon glasses, like a hippy chemist from the sixties. We are led out the back where a huge cauldron sits on a log fire. Inside the pot he stirs and crushes the cactus with a long wooden pestle.

"She'll be done by the end of the day. It'll end up looking like this." He produces a small bottle filled with thick green goo.

"It tastes like shit. Best just swallow, and wash your mouth out with water. Be careful not to vomit, or you'll need another dose."

We are also advised to take it first thing in the morning after a light breakfast to maximise the effect. An appointment is made to come back tomorrow and take it here; the trip is going to last about fourteen hours ...

It's hard to describe in words my first mescaline trip. It comes on slowly as I am taking a shower in the farmhouse, barely perceptibly at first, then before I know it I am lost in a trancelike sea of calm. There is a view out of the window through the flowers and plants, down the hillside, and into the valley of Vilcabamba itself. The setting is idyllic, the lush green valley set amongst brown craggy mountains that are topped with almost perfect triangular peaks. The saturation of the colours are now spectacularly intense, and I am transfixed by every detail while the water falls steadily on my back. Soon every drop that hits my skin, every splash, feels like I'm experiencing it for the first time, as if the sense of feel and touch has somehow eluded me before this day. The constant pitter-patter is both sensuous and hypnotic. Losing all track of time, I stay for hours without a disturbance; it's the longest shower of my life.

In the grounds of the farm are the guest rooms, bamboo huts built rambling up the side of the hill, scattered amongst the vines and the crops. The hammock on my porch has the same stunning views as the farmhouse, and I rest up there to survey the valley. A dog comes and sits opposite me, his eyes staring calmly into mine. His face resembles an old family pet I once loved, and soon the face transforms imperceptibly from one to the other. I talk to this apparition like a reunion with a long lost friend: nostalgia for the good times and regrets for the bad; it feels cathartic and not in the least bit unnatural, but perhaps it's fortunate there is no one to witness it.

Later I discover the real reason for his familiarity with me: a packet of biscuits in my room has been unearthed and hastily eaten. A connection now forged between me and his stomach, this dog impostor will forever be my friend ...

Unfortunately Yishai has not been quite so relaxed, struggling hopelessly against the effects of his trip. He comes to me distressed and paranoid, so I take him to the video hut to watch a film together - the surreal black comedy 'Brazil'. I will never know if a different choice would have affected me as much, but 'Brazil' is now my favourite film of all time.

Later at dinner the conversation is minimal, as guests struggle not only with their appetites, but also with the basic motor skills necessary to lift forks to mouths. Soon a silence permeates, as each of us concentrates on the onerous task of chewing and swallowing with dry throats. Most give up easily and start drifting from the table to their beds, and it's not long before I too join the steady exodus. It has been a long day for everyone ...

Later in my stay I take the cactus once again, but this time the effect is notably reduced; I am unable to reproduce the intensity of the first trip. Yishai and I, though, have become friends, and decide to travel onwards through Ecuador together. We take buses to Baños, a volcanic town where we bathe in the natural hot springs, before heading to the jungle in Mishualli. The beauty of Ecuador lies in its compactness; a half day bus ride can take you from jungle to mountains, or mountains to beach. It is also, like Peru and Bolivia, a colourful country, largely populated by indigenous Indians whose traditional dress and wares adorn every market square.

The hotel in Mishualli has a resident monkey whose facial features are uncannily human, with the wizened detail of an old man. The fixed expression on his face is one of disdain, and it's hard to disagree with this sentiment given the chain that's attached to one of his legs. Yishai and I are here to organise a jungle trek, both for us and for a group of recently arrived English girls who we have decided to joined forces with. Unfortunately the guide we have been recommended is unavailable, and the alternative turns out to be a difficult and unpleasant man; after days of endless negotiations, we decide against doing the trip, and the girls depart without us. We leave the town unsuccessful, though not without a new experience.

Easily available from the street dealers in town is a drug called basuco, a dangerously addictive form of cocaine paste; soaked in kerosine, it's essentially the dregs that remain after the best product has been exported. We've been told that the locals who smoke it become addicted and die young, and it's not hard to see why. The high is enjoyable, but frustratingly short, and the temptation to smoke another joint immediately afterwards is hard to resist. But it's the taste that leaves the most overwhelming impression; like sucking on a car's exhaust, you are constantly reminded of its dangerous toxicity. During one of these smoking sessions, I am admonished by one of the girls:

"Remember what you told me about crouching down to scare away dogs?"

"Ye..es," I say slowly. The idea was from a book I'd read called 'The tropical traveller'. The author maintained that if you crouch down, stray dogs will think you are picking up stones to throw at them.

"Well, it didn't work. I went back to my hotel last night, and that big Alsatian was there again. I crouched down slowly, just like you said ... and it bit me on the nose."

Perhaps I laughed too much at this. It seemed like a reasonable piece of advice to give; but the tables are about to be ruthlessly turned on me ...

Yishai and I head towards the coast next. We are both curious about business opportunities here and plan to check out the beach bars; Yishai is already an entrepreneur of sorts, having made a small fortune from a fashion accessory store in Haifa.

"Jon, you don't understand, it's very easy," he explains in his simple Spanish. "I buy this stuff, very cheap, plastic. The girls love it, they go crazy. Jon, I have an apartment, I have a BMW. It's very easy."

But when we arrive at the hippy resort of Muisne, we are disappointed. The beach is dirty, and all the palm trees have been felled due to a recent outbreak of disease. It's an ugly sight, with fallen trunks as far as the eye can see. And one day as I walk alone down the beach, I am confronted by a pack of stray dogs. There are no stones to pick up here, only sand, and I resort to instinct. I turn my back and walk slowly away, as if undisturbed by the menacing barks and growls. Unfortunately, the smallest and bravest of them senses my fear and bites my ankle from behind. I kick the dog off me, but it's too late; the skin has been broken and blood drawn. Although the odds are unlikely, the spectre of rabies will haunt me now for the next few weeks ...

We relocate to Atacames, a busier and livelier resort further up the coast where the tree devastation hasn't quite reached. On the first night we sample one of the bars built on the sands of the beach, and find ourselves talking to a group of locals on vacation from Quito. One of the girls, unusually blond for an Ecuadorian, shows an interest in me, and we talk for a while at the bar. She suggests we go for a walk and immediately I am sceptical; it has never been this easy for me. As a precaution I walk with her in the opposite direction to the one she suggests, towards the town instead of away. It seems innocent enough, and we sit by a log in the sand smoking a joint and watching the surf break on the shore.

But suddenly two shapes emerge from the darkness and I stand up quickly in reflex. Two tall Africans are upon us, each carrying a long machete. One of them demands money from me, while the other takes the girl aside. I open up my wallet which contains only three or four dollars.

"Dame todo!" he insists, not content with his haul so far.

I extend my arm to offer up my watch, a cheap digital I bought in Peru for a few dollars; my mind is thinking slowly and calmly now, as the effects of the grass begin to take hold. As he fumbles to undo the watch strap with his left hand - his right still holding the machete up high, ready for a swing - I can see over his shoulder that the other two are relaxed and in quiet conversation. Something is not right. She is still wearing her jewellery; no robbery appears to be taking place. Yet despite this apparent collusion, I am still content with the knowledge that my secret is safe. For unbeknown to them, the beach hut where I am staying is too flimsy to leave my cash, and now, in a money belt strapped to my waist, lies a thick wad of twenties that make up nearly three thousand dollars.

Unfortunately, this particular thief is no fool. After pocketing the watch, he frisks me carefully. I can't be sure if he felt the belt, but his next move is ominous. He grabs my T-shirt and pushes me downwards:

"Siente!" he commands - sit down.

But I can sense he has become nervous after standing here for so long, and I have already made my decision; I start crouching in obedience, then quickly spring back up:

"FUCK ... O..F..F!" I scream, pushing him back with all the strength I can summon. His hand is torn from my shirt, and he staggers back nearly six feet. I am ready to turn and run if necessary; there is a lamp post about fifty yards away. But instead he retreats, shocked, and the two of them turn and walk swiftly away. Immediately the adrenalin surges, bringing an overwhelming compulsion to give chase. Instead, I check myself, and repeat the blood curdling scream:

"FUCK ... O..F..F!"

For me it's a momentous victory. Back at the bar in my ripped T-shirt, I feel like a returning hero, while the girl seeks solace with her friends, crying conspicuously. But she is an appalling actress; her tearless wailing is melodramatic, almost comical. I say to her cruelly:

"Tell your friends I had three thousand in my belt. Tell them what they missed."

Yishai, on the other hand, is laughing:

"Que hora es?" he asks, pointing to my now empty wrist. He had grown used to me showing off my watch and boasting how good it was for the few dollars I paid for it. Now that it's gone, he will spend the next few weeks forever asking me the time.

As expected, a visit to this country would not be complete without an obligatory stay in its capital, Quito. With a pretty colonial centre full of whitewash architecture, narrow cobbled streets and colourful markets, it is one of the best preserved old towns in South America. However, it is the ugly modern part of the city that Yishai decides to devote most of his time to; for in the gaudily lit basement of a large soulless chain hotel, Yishai is beginning to develop a gambling habit.

Casinos seem to be a feature of every major Ecuadorian town, and we have already sampled one on a stopover from the coast. Now Yishai is visiting the casino every night, sitting at the roulette table for several hours at a time, entranced by the spinning wheel. He returns in the early hours to announce a profit or loss, his eyes bloodshot and exhausted:

"Jon, I won six hundred dollars."

"Jon, I lost three hundred."

It's a roller-coaster ride that has me increasingly concerned for my new friend; these sums are far too big for a traveller with only one or two grand to his name. Every day I urge him to quit while he's ahead; then evening duly comes, and the temptation is too great once again.

And while this struggle continues, a water shortage in Quito is making our hotel less and less habitable. We are able to take sporadic showers, but the toilets soon become blocked; worst of all, the residents - ladies and gentlemen alike - resort to defecating on the floor next to the bowl, which is now full to the brim. It's a sight that will prove hard to erase from my subconscious. But it's also a stick to beat my friend with, slowly and surely, into submission; for it's time for us to leave this town now. The next stop on our itinerary is a country both beautiful and dangerous in equal measure. We are heading north to Columbia ...

Although Columbia has a reputation for drug related violence, we have been told that most of this is concentrated around Medellín in the west of the country. So we set off to travel the eastern route through the Magdalena Valley, heading ultimately for the north coast and the Caribbean Sea.

Perched near the head of the valley, San Agustin is a pretty terracotta-roofed town where a lost civilisation from the thirteenth century has left tall free-standing statues scattered in the nearby hills, similar to the more famous ones of Easter Island. The characters sculpted in stone resemble the primitive icons used in early computer games, and they are now maintained in neat fenced-off gardens for the benefit of the visiting tourists. We decide to stay on a ramshackle farm run by a Swiss immigrant and his Columbian wife, who grow coffee as a cash crop and rent out a few rooms to travellers to break even. At first they mistake us for the citizens of some obscure South American country; this is quite common now - the pidgin Spanish that we use to communicate sounds fluent, but is mostly unintelligible to outsiders. When a word is unknown to us, we simply replace it with "esa cosa que ..." - the thing that - followed by a quick explanation or mime, like an old-fashioned parlour game; sometimes the unknown word is replaced with something similar but close enough. As a result, we can talk with a minimal vocabulary on a multitude of topics. It works remarkably well. And with this new language we speak freely with our hosts, curious about the alternative lifestyle that tempts so many Westerners desperate to leave the rat race. For them the answer is simple: "It's a constant struggle. The farmers here are crushed. Every year the crop prices go down. But for us, this life ..." He waves his arm at the surrounding countryside. "It's worth it."

On our way north from San Agustin we rest only briefly in the capital Bogotá, where bombings are a daily threat; just a walk down the street can be fraught when you're wondering which parked car might explode at any moment. We stop long enough to replace my stolen watch though, another three dollar digital bargain. And now that I can recount the time once more, I do so on a regular basis, much to the annoyance of Yishai.

When we reach Santa Marta on the Caribbean coast, we head straight to the Tayrona national park just west of the town, a large conservation area by the sea. In a small village on the outskirts of the park we hire a donkey to carry our bags through the forest, and after a few hours trek, we arrive at a beautiful sandy cove with large polished rocks strewn along the margins of the beach. It's unspoilt and deserted, apart from a few wooden shacks housing the local coconut traders. In one of these houses there are six hammocks for rent, and we get the last two, sharing with two Danish girls and a Scottish couple. It's a stunning spot, and we decide to stay for several days.

There are many empty beaches on this stretch of coast, and in the next bay we are able to cast away our clothes and skinny dip in the sea with a feeling of complete isolation. Every evening at dusk we play football with the locals, after which they cook dinner for us with whatever provisions came in on the donkey that day. They are even adept at devising their own cocktail, a drink made with fermented pineapple juice and tasting exactly like a pina colada. It's a simple and easy existence, with something of the Robinson Crusoe about it. But on the fourth day, the Scottish girl falls sick. She has lain too long on the beach on an overcast afternoon, and the sun has burnt her easily through the clouds. Her skin is bright red and painful to the touch, and she has been vomiting; no amount of aftersun cream can help her now, and we decide to have her stretchered out by four of the locals. She is on her way to hospital.

And soon we too make our exit from this paradise. On our way to Cartagena, we stop briefly to watch a football match in the international stadium in Baranquilla - a world cup qualifier between Columbia and Israel. Yishai is the only Israeli supporter in sight, and I am prepared to switch allegiance at any moment, but the Columbian fans are surprisingly friendly and buy us beer throughout the match. Although the result is a disappointing 1-0 win for the home team, the camaraderie with the locals leaves a lasting impression.

When we reach Cartagena, it is with some sadness on my part. This will be my last port of call in South America before I fly to Miami; I have reached the end of the continent. It is, nevertheless, something of a jewel in the crown. A well preserved fortress city dating back to the sixteenth century, it still maintains the colonial air of its past, with narrow winding streets and overhanging balconies. But like Quito, it wouldn't be complete without its modern centre and its tempting array of casinos; Yishai, now perilously low on funds, gambles for his ticket to Miami ..... and wins. I escort him to the travel agent immediately afterwards ...

On the day before our flight out, we take a boat trip to the Rosario Islands, an archipelago not far from the city. There we find hundreds of small islands with properties built on them, many only large enough for a single house. We are told that most of these belong to the drug kingpins, with one in particular belonging to the most powerful of all - Pablo Escobar, a man soon to come to a sticky end. We swim by the side of our boat in the warm shallow waters, with his infamous floating mansion as our backdrop, a reminder of the riches made from one of Columbia's biggest exports. It seems a fitting way to finish my journey through South America.

But there is an epilogue to this story, like the resurgent henchman in the last minutes of a Bond movie. A final lesson to mark my trip.

We decide to stop off in the Columbian owned island of San Andrés en route to Miami. It's a free stopover, and this tiny island just off the coast of Nicaragua is an ex-British colony offering some of the atmosphere of the Caribbean. The main town sits next to the airport, surrounded by white coral beaches, coconut palms and clear turquoise seas. Oddly, the majority of businesses here are shops selling duty-free goods to Columbian holiday makers, many stocked with items as unwieldy as fridges and washing machines.

We stay at the Restrepo, a hotel that has its own permanent residents of Jamaican fishermen. Many of them lounge around in hammocks telling their stories in the evenings, and one in particular is a legend amongst travellers - a notorious stowaway who travels the world by jumping on and off cargo ships. Naturally, in these Jamaican-inhabited surroundings, it's not too difficult to score some grass.

One evening after the sun goes down, we decide to share a joint on the beach before heading back to the hotel. Sitting by the shore, lost in conversation, we hardly notice the long shadows creeping up from behind us. Instinctively I bury the roach in the sand and turn around quickly. Four policemen wielding batons, now with voices raised, are on top of us. Amongst the ensuing chaos, I hold up my cigarette packet:

"Cigarrillos!" I protest.

But they are not buying the story. Instead, one shines a torch onto the sand as the other three search for the evidence on their hands and knees. And then suddenly there it is, poking out of the sand, disturbed by a sifting hand. I see it first, but the policeman with the torch immediately follows my line of sight. I have to act quickly. In a moment of panic, I run and kick sand everywhere like a crazed lunatic ...

It's hard to say if this rush to the head has made matters better or worse; I've managed to lose the evidence, but now we are beaten heavily with sticks and marched into the back of their police van. As we are driven off, I remind Yishai of the danger we are in: sitting on one of the beds in our hotel room, plain for all to see, is a bag full of grass; if they ask to search the room, we'll be in far bigger trouble. My fears, however, are temporarily allayed. When we reach the police station, the chief has gone home; and instead of being interrogated, we are thrown in jail to await judgement in the morning.

The night is interminably long. We are in a six by six foot cell with five other prisoners, and there is no room to lie down. Our fellow detainees seem to be here for one of two reasons: for being drunk and disorderly, or for taking a short cut home across the airport runway. And I have a particular discomfort that I divulge to Yishai. When the police beat me earlier, I had an involuntary loosening of the bowels. If I sit down now, I will be sitting in my own shit. The morning can't come fast enough.

But Yishai is far more distressed than I am. It's unclear exactly why, but he mentions his time in the Israeli army when he served in a tank division; it seems he just can't tolerate being locked up. And just after dawn, he shouts to the guards to let us out. I try to calm him down, but it's impossible; when they continue to ignore him, he starts hurling insults:

"Idiotas! Hijos de putas! Abri la puerta!"

Moments later, two of them enter the cell and beat him up. It's brutal, and I can only watch. After a two hour wait I am released from the cell, but Yishai is pushed back inside, the guards taking an obvious pleasure in telling him he is going nowhere. Unfortunately Yishai's ordeal is set to continue.

Brought before the police chief, I prepare myself for an interrogation, determined to feign ignorance of the name of my hotel. Instead, he asks me why I am there:

"I don't know," I lie in my broken Spanish. "We were just smoking cigarettes on the beach. I don't know why we were arrested."

He thinks for a minute. It appears he doesn't actually know the reason. Those policemen must be off-shift now.

"Clean the garden," he instructs. "Follow that man over there, he will show you."

I am led outside the police station and handed a plastic bag for collecting litter. With the airport jaywalker to help me, the narrow strip of grass is clean in less than thirty minutes, and I am duly released. I rush back to the hotel with an increasingly nervous energy, until I reach the room and quickly dispose of the evidence. It's only then that I can breathe a huge sigh of relief ...

For the next few days I bring food to Yishai in prison. He is still crazed and out of control, and they have beaten him again and again in retaliation to more of his insults. His face becomes haunted, and later, defeated. After the third night, they finally let him go. Unsurprisingly perhaps, we take the next available flight out.

17. loads a money

I am panicking now, as the second policeman moves his hands towards the third shelf. Just like those dangers in Ecuador and Columbia, an intervention is desperately needed here - a scream and a push, or a kick of the sand. It's now or never.

"Actually, there is a problem," I say to the policeman counting my money. They all stop what they are doing and listen intently.

"There's a twenty pound note in that pile that I didn't declare. I'm sorry, it was a mistake. It was sent in a birthday card to Nairobi, let me show you."

I walk over to the wardrobe, past the second policeman, who steps out of the way. As I extricate a pile of letters and cards from one of the shelves, I push the newspaper and grass as far as I can into the back of the cupboard out of view. The birthday card is real enough, but there was never any money in it. I flash them a humorous greeting card that I received from my one of my family.

"See, I was too lazy to declare it," I lie, "Perhaps I could pay the fine now? I don't want to make this a big deal."

There is a moment here where once again my fortunes lie on a knife edge, when I'm unsure if the distraction will work. But slowly they begin to relax. The second policeman steps away from the wardrobe; he is not resuming his search, he is now only interested in his prize. I quickly suggest an amount, anything to get them out of my house:

"It seems unfair to confiscate the whole twenty, it was a present after all. How about we split it down the middle, ten pounds each?"

They seem content with this. I pay them in local shillings, and they leave in good spirits, smiles all around. I imagine them clinking beer bottles later that evening after an easy days work.

And Jamila and I soon work out the source of their tip, gleaned from the whispered conversations of the police during the search. The man who had shown me around the vacant land lots in Watamu had asked me if I had the money to buy; of course I claimed that I did, though never that it was in cash, or that the money was in the country. That assumption, or gamble, was his when he tipped off the police - presumably because it had brought him success before. But like my dalliance with business in Peru, it is hard to know who to trust. If I hadn't been told, I never would have guessed that the estate agent was the instigator of the raid. It seems impossible now to do business in a country like this. It feels like the end of a dream ...

After the cash ran out on that long South American adventure, I returned to London. Miami had proved a difficult place to find work, and both Yishai and I had quickly given up trying; America seemed empty and hollow after our recent exploits, and barely worth the effort. But back in England, the economy was thriving under Thatcher; 'loads a money' was now a popular catchphrase, and it seemed as if all the cockney barrow boys had become stock market traders overnight.

It is in this climate that I decide to contact a furniture company I worked for just before my South American trip. I offer to drive for them cash-in-hand at a lower rate than the agency normally charges, but at a higher rate than I usually earn. I'm in luck; they tell me I can start the very next day.

It's a small company importing luxury furniture from Italy and Spain, catering to the burgeoning demands of the aspirational middle classes. We set up installations in the major department stores such as Harrods and Selfridges, and deliver all over the country, both to stores and to people's homes. It's a satisfying and varied job, and on occasion two of us go on trips up north for three or four days. The company pays for all of our expenses, including hotels, and we enjoy a night on the tiles in a different town every night. As the months go by I get to see more of England and Wales than I've seen before in my entire life.

But the work can be back breaking. The biggest seller is a marble table whose top weighs over a hundred kilos. It's unusual to have to take one up several flights of stairs, but it happens nonetheless; and over time, like the biceps I developed 'on the dust', my forearms become as thick as my calves. It's an odd sensation, as they become almost disconnected from the rest of my body.

And there are many tricks of the trade to be learnt from this high-end business. One of our tasks is to install glass wall units in our customer's living rooms. This being the eighties, the finish is almost always in black veneer, so a quick surreptitious swipe of a black felt-tip pen will cover any scuff mark that occurs along the way; it's as important a part of our toolkit as a screwdriver. And the exorbitant prices of our merchandise mean that we often have demanding customers; the psychology of this requires that we carry a spare table top on the van, allowing them to swap one out if they don't like the particular pattern of the marble. On one occasion the spare is missing, and I redeliver the very same table off the back of the van, back to front. It's happily accepted.

Meanwhile, I am working hard in the busy lead up to Christmas. With overtime every weekday and double time on Saturdays, I am saving enough money each week to travel for a month. I am happy - it's a ratio I have never managed to achieve before. And now I have something to look forward to as well; when business slacks off in the new year, I can take time off, with a visit to an old friend in the works. In fact, a familiar looking typewritten letter has recently landed on my doormat:

Dear fellow proffesor and honoured collegue

Thanks for the latest report and experiences of S-Amerika. Very interesting and valuable information for generations to come. The next thing might come as some kind of a shock, and I'm aware it might even lose my title and good reputation. A week ago I got my appartment in this sleepy town called Purmerend, I also took my girlfriend with me. Sorry to dissapoint you but this is not all. About 6 months ago I stopped smoking dope because I was going completely mad. After being back in Holland I moved in with my sister and we smoked 100 grams in one month and of course a lot of booze to get rid of the dry mouth. At the end I was so paranoid that I hardly left the house. Also I have been working for the last 4 months as a driver. It doesn't pay much but it's fun. It is all second hand furniture, so I have first choice in what to take, I got this appartment filled up with all this shit for free! (including Stereo, TV and fridge) Fuck, you probably think I turned completely to some materialistic shit-house, but as long as it's free I don't give a fuck.

I was wondering what you had in mind for christmas, if you would like you should come around for a while because there is lot's of room. Ive got the week off and because I take my van home I could show you around a bit beside's getting pissed a lot, and meeting some of my mates. So let me know as soon as possible.

Christ so much space left and I already don't have anything to say because there is hardly anything happening over here beside some fighting or stabbing occasionaly. A couple of months ago some skinhead stabbed a mate of mine in his throat and stomach, this same fucking skinhead already did some years for killing a young black guy, anyway the whole pub was getting upset and tried to lynch the motherfucker, it just looked like some old western, the skinhead in his big brand new Volvo and all this people trying to get him out, some how the cops got him out only with some minor damage. His car got completely wrecked and they had to tow it away. Beside this kind of things not much happens here so I stop hammering away on this stupid machine (also free from work) and hope to hear from you soon,

Pisshead KURT
p.s. DIDNT GAVE UP THE DRINKING AND NEVER WILL!!!!!!!!!!

I do make it to Purmerend, but not until after the new year, when the eighties have already crept furtively into the nineties. Kurt is somewhat subdued during my stay, sleeping and rising early each day to go to work. I spend the cold wintery days roaming the streets of Amsterdam, and the evenings smoking and drinking in his flat. It is great to catch up with Kurt after all this time, but there appears to be little prospect of travelling together again; it has taken him over a year to secure an apartment and job, and finally get back on his feet. Unsurprisingly perhaps, he is reluctant to give it all up.

And back In London, I am soon reacquainted with Stacey. I meet her new husband in their flat in Hackney where we smoke a few joints together and listen to music. I will see Stacey many times over the years, and we are destined to become good friends again; but like Kurt, her life has now taken a different course.

And so it is that after a further six months of delivering marble tables, amassing another tidy sum to set me on my way, I decide to take up an invitation from somewhere else. Yishai owns a flat next to the beach in Haifa and has asked me to come over for a visit. It's nearing the end of summer, and the timing seems just right. Without much thought of where I might end up, I pack my bag once again.

18. the fifth journey

My first impressions of Israel are not good. In fact my opinion is formed before I am even able to leave Heathrow airport. After I arrive at the check-in desk, I am hastily escorted into a back room for interrogation by the airline security staff. The woman that conducts the interview is a particularly nasty piece of work; she continually questions my integrity, then scoffs at my answers:

"Why are you flying El-Al?"

"Because it was the cheapest flight."

"That's a lie."

"Errrr .... no. Actually, it's true ..."

We get into a particularly heated exchange about my radio cassette. She had asked me if I was carrying anything electronic in my bag, to which I had answered in the negative. What she had meant by this, but didn't clarify, was the hold luggage surreptitiously being searched next door, not the carry-on bag I have with me.

"Why did you lie about the radio?"

"I didn't lie, I misunderstood you."

For ten minutes we argue the semantics of her question. I point out that I am the one more likely to have a better grasp of the English language. But it's not the end of the inquisition; next, my relationship to Yishai is called into doubt with a range of paranoid hypotheses:

"How do you know he is what he says he is? ..."

"How do you know he's not a terrorist? ..."

"What will you do if he isn't at the airport to meet you? Where will you go? ..."

It is hard to give coherent responses to all these questions, but I do my best. Eventually I am allowed on the plane, though by that point I no longer wish to fly; the only thing stopping me from asking for a refund is my obligation to keep a rendezvous with Yishai. Once on board, I find out that most of the foreign nationals have suffered a similar interrogation. Needless to say, they have made their point; though not advertised as such, El Al is exclusively for the Israelis ...

Yishai's apartment resides in a low rise development in the north Haifan suburb of Kiryat Yam. It is, as promised, only a few minutes from a beach that stretches flat and wide to almost each horizon. And for something so recently built, the resort has a clear sense of community; every day after dusk, the main thoroughfare is busy with families parading up and down on an evening walk, while the less energetic line the benches people-watching. Yishai's flat, however, is curiously sparse, like a holiday home that's been recently vacated. The kitchen in particular shows no signs of habitation, with the fridge revealing only three lonely occupants, each of them abandoned long ago. Instead we eat at his mother's house, a short drive away, in a family tradition that often draws in his brothers and sisters from the surrounding suburbs.

And Yishai is an enthusiastic host. I am taken to the best kebab shop in Haifa where, with strict attention to detail, we arrive at the precise time of day when the meat is at its tenderest. On another day, he takes me gliding at a nearby kibbutz, where he shows off his prowess as a pilot by taking our glider up through the thermals in ever tighter circles. My experience as a passenger, however, is less than spectacular; I spend most of the stomach-churning flight fending off the urge to vomit.

After a week in Haifa, we set off in Yishai's famed BMW for a quick tour of the country. I had once been told that in Israel you can be led for miles by its eager residents just to show you the slow trickle of a tiny waterfall; in a country as arid as this, water is a rare and prized commodity. So I am not surprised when I am taken to the largest expanses of these by my host. First we enjoy the lively town of Tiberias, that sits on the shore of Lake Galilee with distant views across the water to the West Bank. Then we drive down to the Dead Sea, where we float in surreal suspension, half-in, half-out of the heavily salted water. It's an odd but pleasant sensation, spoilt only by the thick greasy layer of sun oil left behind by its previous occupants.

And finally we end up in Eilat, a popular resort at the southern tip of Israel which nestles on a short strip of coast by the Red Sea. Despite the small footprint, the area has been utilised to maximum effect. The snorkelling is surprisingly good - with little effort, we find hundreds of species of reef fish in the shallow coral next to the main beach; while further down the coast, an underwater aquarium built into a bank of submerged coral allows a scuba-eye view without getting wet.

The atmosphere of the town centre is eclectic, with travellers hostels rubbing shoulders with the rich resorts, but it is the seedier side that ends up marring our stay. We are drinking quietly in an English pub one night, when a drunk decides to pick a fight with Yishai for spurious reasons: offence was apparently caused when he pushed a dog away that was threatening to knock over our beer. With a large group of friends behind him, he punches Yishai hard in the face. It's a cowardly act; we are clearly outnumbered and cannot respond. And of course, the idiot who has just assaulted my generous host is in fact British, a compatriot of mine. The shame that I feel in this moment is complete.

It is also, sadly, one of Yishai's last days with me; we have already made plans to part ways after this trip, and he duly drops me near Jerusalem to continue on my journey. I spend three days exploring its labyrinthian streets on foot. It's a fascinating and controversial city with historical significance to three major religions, and the character and atmosphere of the various quarters reflect this complex dynamic. But after extensive photography and some very tired feet, I am ready to move on. I have decided to make use of my geographical proximity and pay a visit to an equally important place in the events of ancient history - Egypt.

But despite three pleasant weeks in Israel, the security services will have the last laugh: unbeknown to me, my unexposed rolls of film carried in the luggage hold from London have already been ruined by an Xray machine in Tel Aviv airport. All the photos that I've framed and shot so carefully during my stay in Israel are over-exposed. None of them will survive.

Cairo is like a change of worlds. Arriving from a country where so much is newly built and rising, this city seems to be old and falling down. It's an impression gained from a general neglect of the building facades and the amount of rubble that litters the rooftops. And it's loud. The Egyptian style of driving involves tooting the horn at everyone and everything that gets in the way; there are no apparent rules for right of way, just the crazed whistles of policemen conducting traffic at the busy junctions. But therein lies its charm; this is a chaotic city, but one that's most definitely alive.

Only a short and hectic bus ride from the centre of Cairo lie the historic Pyramids of Giza, and when I first arrive, I am completely taken aback. From the many photos I have seen, I never would have guessed how close they are to the city; the sphinx sits gazing over a sprawling suburb only a few hundred yards from its outstretched paws, barely staving off the invasion of this new civilisation. Yet it's impossible to be unimpressed by the scale of this site. From a distance the pyramids seem smooth in outline, but walk closer and the jagged edge of their rectangular block construction soon becomes apparent; once you are upon them, those tiny blocks are now as tall as you. The illusion of that perfect geometric shape is broken just as the extraordinary endeavour that built them is revealed.

And it's easy to spend a lot of time here. You can find your own space just by walking a few hundred yards into the desert, where yet another spectacular perspective on the pyramids can be found; and everywhere you go, a short inspection of the sand beneath your feet reveals the smaller remnants of Egyptian history - pieces of broken pottery likely thousands of years old, and so abundant that they are regularly trodden underfoot and barely even noticed ...

Although Cairo has far more than just the pyramids to offer, I decide to head south immediately in the knowledge that I will soon return. The local train to Luxor has three classes, and I choose the middle one; it's uncomfortable and crowded and, later I discover, dangerous. There are fans mounted to the ceiling to cool the carriages, and early on in the journey a man rushes through our car with blood pouring out of a wound in his head; one of them has apparently worked its way loose. I look at the fan above my own head, rattling crazily with a few loose screws holding it in place, and quickly move seats across the aisle ...

Luxor has a host of historic sights in close proximity, and I manage to visit most of them during my stay. I particularly savour the massive columns of Karnak, so closely spaced that it's easy to lose yourself amongst them, and the statues of Abu Simbel, carved twenty metres tall out of a cliff face near the Sudanese border. But after several days, I tire of the endless temples, statues and obelisks, and decide to venture off piste. In the Valley of the Kings, only a few hundred yards from the tomb of Tutankhamun, lie hundreds of lesser known tombs, all bricked up, but each potentially offering untold Indiana-Jones-style adventures. I pick one of these at random with a hole just big enough for me to climb through. A tunnel leads down at about forty-five degrees and, armed with a torch, I scramble down the stony incline into the pitch blackness. When I reach the bottom, I discover a network of tunnels just big enough to crawl through leading in multiple directions. I choose one to follow, then descend deeper into the rabbit warren until the passage ends in a small empty chamber. And there I discover my prize: amongst the dirt and the rubble, I find one small identifiable object - a torn piece of mummy bandage. These tombs have been repeatedly looted over the centuries until nothing remains, but this small memento is more than enough for me.

Back at my hostel dormitory, I am disturbed in my sleep by a noisy and inconsiderate German returning late at night. I am further put out when my admonishment is rudely ignored, but on the following day I notice there is something unusual about my new roommate. After a few failed attempts at attracting his attention once again, the penny drops; he is deaf. In an instant my feelings of contempt turn to those of admiration, and with a mime that is easily interpreted internationally, I invite him out for a beer that evening. Although we have no language in common, I have spent months honing my skills with Yishai in South America, and the conversation is conducted through the crude medium of mime. He turns out to be fascinating company. Hailing from Munich and still in his early twenties, he has undertaken this trip against the wishes of his family and is travelling completely alone. It's not the first time he has ventured forth; last year he set off by himself on a cycling tour of Europe. But he explains to me how, sadly, his disability often makes him unapproachable; nights out such as this with a fellow traveller are a rare event. I wonder how he manages in a country where he can neither hear, read nor speak the language, and later in the evening I witness his technique as he buys cigarettes from a street trader. I signal to him that I'm impressed, but that unfortunately he's been taken advantage of and has paid way over the odds. He dismisses this with a shrug; this is of little concern to him. And straight away I get it: it's not about the money. Being here is achievement enough.

After a brief trip to Aswan and a dhow trip along the Nile, I return to Cairo once again in a state of limbo. I visit the Egyptian Museum, one of the best in the world, which houses so many of the mummies rescued from the tombs of Luxor, in particular the most famous and elaborate one of all - Tutankhamun. And I wander through the eerie City of The Dead, a four mile strip of tombs and mausoleums built to house the recent dead, but which is now cohabited by many of the living. Then one day when I return to the dormitory in my hotel, there sits across from me a newly arrived, lightly bearded Englishman. He hails from Andover, and his name is Neil.

We hit it off straight away. Neil has just returned from a solo trek down the east bank of the Nile by camel, an animal that he bought in the market at Luxor, then sold off at the end of his trip. The camel was a nightmare to handle, grumpy and obstreperous, but he managed a few hundred miles nonetheless. Inspired by this sense of adventure, we decide to explore Cairo's seedier side together. In the daytime, it's the shisha dens that we are drawn to; this is where the older, wiser looking locals sit smoking tobacco and molasses through giant water pipes whilst playing backgammon. We challenge them to games, but find it hard to keep up with the speed; we can only beat them if we slow down to our own pedestrian pace. Meanwhile, the tobacco gives a pleasant high, like the first cigarette that you ever smoked. We soon become connoisseurs of these spots, rating the ambience and the quality of the smoke, and we wonder if a book should be written in the manner of a Michelin Guide.

Then in the evenings we sample the bars. Egypt does not really have a drinking culture, and the bars that we find are underground and squalid, hidden in the darkest alleyways of the city. But the process of rooting them out is an adventure itself, and a guidebook is touted in similar fashion, perhaps to be combined with the previous.

The most interesting one we find is at a belly dancing venue. We are served beer like champagne, in flamboyant ice buckets at the side of our table, as a grotesque show unfolds in front of us. First the acrobats: young girls performing cartwheels and somersaults, then contorting their bodies as the audience politely clap each twisted pose. The belly dancers follow with a few simple dances, slowly leading up to the grand finale, when the star of the show is ceremoniously revealed. On to the stage comes a grossly unattractive woman with clumsily dyed blond hair, performing her fat wobbling trick to the delights of the ogling Egyptian men. They stuff banknotes into her sarong like punters in a strip club. Soon the men at the front storm the stage uninvited, wiggling their big stomachs alongside her with a far better rhythm and technique. It's so over the top that we are seized by an uncontrollable fit of the giggles.

But during this guidebook research we have also been doing some serious planning. Considering an overland trip south, we have made several chaotic visits to the Sudanese embassy to obtain visas, only to be told that our applications will take three months to process due to an ongoing civil war. Although this rules out an overland journey, we have decided to travel to central Africa nevertheless, after sourcing a cheap flight to Nairobi. My fifth journey has taken an unexpected turn ...

I return to Kenya with fond memories of my first visit, and it greets me with the familiarity of an old friend. Neil, however, has only passed through briefly before and is keen to go on safari straight away. Having both experienced commercial safaris in the past, the one we endeavour to organise this time is a little more adventurous: do it yourself. We hire a four wheel drive Suzuki for a week from a small local business, sharing the cost with a third traveller, Saskia, an East German girl from our hostel. The following day we drive to the Masai Mara armed with our tents and provisions, but as night draws in, a flat tyre forces us to pull over at the side of the road near the park entrance. Camping next to the car in the driving rain, we are woken in the night by the roar of lions. With no protection other than a thin layer of canvas, it's a terrifying sound, but I assure myself they are far away; a roar can carry for miles, yet still sound like it's right next to you. Saskia, though, wisely moves out of her tent and into the car.

The next day we find a far better place to camp, next to a research station in the middle of the park; although not officially sanctioned, we manage to get permission from one of the rangers. At night we light a fire which keeps on burning to the early hours, and although the lions can be heard once again, I sleep soundly with the knowledge of our deterrent. In the morning we wake groggily to find a herd of giraffe grazing at a nearby tree; it's a serene and captivating scene, and we all eat our breakfasts in silent appreciation.

In the daytime it's easy to find game here; this famous park has one of the biggest concentrations of wildlife in Africa. Around every corner lies a herd or a pride, and we have no need to follow the hoards of minibuses that flock to surround every cheetah or lion; instead we venture away from the convoys and find our own space. We have been fortunate enough to catch the tail end of the migration season, and the plains are now full of wandering wildebeest as far as the eye can see. Our car is old, however, and we break down frequently. Most commonly there's a loose connection with the battery, and I soon become adept at jiggling the wires under the bonnet to fix it - though not before I've carefully scanned every nearby bush for any signs of danger ...

On our return to Nairobi, we are forced to review our plans for Central Africa. It appears we are heading there for the rainy season when the roads will be impassable, and it would be much wiser if we delayed the start of our journey. After a particularly long session at the infamous Modern Green Bar in Latema Road, we come up with a neat solution: we will take time out on the Kenyan Coast to do a bit of scuba diving ....

19. gorillas

As Neil and I sit silently in the train heading for the Ugandan border, I am in sombre mood. I have just hugged my goodbyes to Jamila and Otto on the station platform, and already have an acute empty feeling in the pit of my stomach. But I have promised to return in a few months time, and I convince myself that I will soon draw comfort from that fact.

We switch trains at the border to continue to Kampala and are immediately immersed in our new world. The windows of the carriage we now occupy are spattered with bullet holes, grouped as if for target practice, and we wonder if the war in the north has ever come this far south. President Museveni has brought renewed hope to Uganda since coming to power five years ago, but it's still very much a country in recovery mode, and the fight with rebels in the north persists. The Asians, however, are slowly returning to reclaim their businesses after being banished by Idi Amin in the seventies, and with them comes the promise of an upturn in the economy. It should be a relatively upbeat time to visit this sadly impoverished country.

Soon though, we are reminded of what lies ahead. Our train breaks down on a remote stretch of track, and we wait five hours for an engineer to arrive by bus to fix the problem. By the time we reach Kampala, night has long since fallen, and we emerge from the station unsure of where to stay; having had little tourism over the last twenty years, there are few operational hotels in the capital apart from the upmarket Hilton. In fact, on inspection, there appears to be very little of anything that is operational, with most buildings boarded up or abandoned.

And so we take a shared taxi way out into the suburbs, heading for a hostel that we're told may still have rooms. There we find not a hotel, but a school that rents out its classrooms in the evenings to travellers. A thin sponge mattress is handed to each of us by the janitor, as he explains to us the rules: we have to be out by eight in the morning, ready for the school day to begin, with our bags and mattresses locked away in a cupboard; we can then return after five o'clock to sleep. Having no real choice in the matter, we agree to the arrangement, joining desks to make our ad hoc beds for the night ...

Seeing it for the first time in daylight, the centre of Kampala has an air of the apocalypse about it. Above the ghost-town parades of long gone businesses perch an army of Marabou storks, who stand silently observing the human population from the tops of broken lamp posts and telegraph poles. At first sight, they look like vultures ready to pounce on the inhabitants at the merest sign of fatigue; the scene is not far from how I would imagine the end of civilisation. But away from the centre the markets are thriving, as if a new population is encroaching on the old, ready to reinvigorate an abandoned city.

Evidence of Uganda's twenty year decay can also be found in its currency, with inflation spiralling out of control. The largest denomination available is a one hundred shilling note, which is only worth about two English pence. This makes money counting a national pastime. When we change twenty pounds, we get an unwieldy six inch pile of notes, and when the local businessmen come to the bank, they bring empty cardboard boxes to carry away their spoils. But Neil and I have developed a system to cope with the arithmetic of these large numbers. A folded note containing nine notes we call a wedge; ten wedges tied with an elastic band we call a wad; and ten wads tied up with criss-crossed bands we call a bundle. With this system a wedge is twenty pence, a wad is two pounds, and a bundle is twenty; thus a packet of cigarettes simply costs two wedges. We soon calculate that, although the hundred shilling note is a little too valuable to be wiping our arses with, there are, however, tens in circulation that work out far more economical than toilet paper ...

Kasese is our next port of call, a town that will act as the base for our main objective in coming to Uganda. This largely unremarkable place, with its grid-like layout of single story blocks and muddy streets, has a higher purpose for us: from here we can organise a trek to the Rwenzori Mountains. Also know as the mountains of the moon, this small cluster of snow capped peaks rises to over five thousand meters in the very heart of Africa. They remained undiscovered during the early expeditions of the nineteenth century, largely because they are almost permanently covered in clouds. Ominously, the local name for them translates as 'the hills where the clouds boil'; one thing we know for sure is that we're going to get wet.

Unwilling to risk my shoes in this deluge, I perhaps foolishly decide to borrow a pair of wellington boots from our guide just before we set off. And after a long climb on the first day up a steep narrow path through the muddy forest floor, we finally arrive at our first hut to stop for the night. By now though, not only do I have blisters on each foot, but my feet are soaked through after falling from a log into a fast running stream along the way; no doubt the poor tread of the wellingtons were responsible for the slip. And despite wearing waterproof jacket and trousers, this defence too was easily breached by the incessant rain. And so I arrive, soaked to the bone, top to toe. Yet after a day's punishing climb laden with heavy backpacks, the simple pleasure of removing boots and changing to dry clothes is reward enough. A stove fire and hot food on top of that is beyond bliss.

In the morning, however, the hardest task of the day has to be faced: the swap from a warm dry set of clothes to the cold wet ones from the day before. With the temperatures close to freezing and the stoves unlit, there is a crazed dance and rhythmic grunt that accompanies this ritual, a desperate attempt to get the blood flowing. It's a strong incentive to get going; it takes at least half an hour of walking before the body temperature returns to normal.

On the second day, our hike brings us into our first encounter with bogs. Although there has been an attempt to build wooden walkways across them, most are submerged or broken, and we are forced to pick our way through the muddy expanse. It is not uncommon to sink up to our waist when stepping in the wrong place, requiring our guide to hastily pull us free. But soon after this challenge, we are rewarded with the first sightings of why we are here. Surprisingly perhaps, the main reason we have come to this remote wilderness is to see the flora ...

I had heard it spoken about before, but it's another thing to see it; this is as close to an alien landscape as I will ever experience. The vegetation that grows here seems not of this earth; giant flowers that grow six metres tall, plants that resemble barrel-sized pineapples, and trees dripping with moss that hang in thick clumps off the branches. It's both exotic and surreal. Being alone as we are in this landscape, it's easy to imagine yourself as the explorer of a new world; the best set designers in Hollywood would be in awe of this science fiction paradise.

But it is the altitude and rainfall that make this place so special, and as such it is often an inhospitable environment. We are lucky then, on the third day, when the sun breaks loose. The setting for this fine weather is the best yet, with our hut sitting next to a beautiful lake nestling amongst the snow-capped peaks. We are now at the highest camp on this trek, nearing the pass that will take us down the other side of the mountains. The following day, when we finally reach the snow line, we encounter a vast moraine, it's jumbled pile of rocks blocking our way at the bottom of a glacier. As I clamber clumsily over the slippery surfaces, I contemplate the danger of being stranded here with a broken leg so far from civilisation. But I do not dwell too long on this thought; we are on our descent now, and the relief from the pain of my blisters is only two days away ...

The hotel in Kasese serves conveniently as a convalescence home for my feet. Four of my toes are bloody and raw, and I stay more or less horizontal for three days to allow them to heal. In my suffering I curse Neil, whose idea it was to do this trek in the first place. Back in Nairobi, he had pleaded with me:

"Come on, it's going to be hard, but it'll be worth it."

"What's the point of getting cold, wet and miserable for five days, just to say you've done it?" I complained.

"Come on, I've heard amazing things about this place. I'm going to do it anyway, but it'll be much better with the two of us."

His argument eventually won out. He is far more adventurous than me, and like the scuba diving in Watamu, I was happy to be pulled along in the slipstream. But now, as the blisters begin to heal, I realise that he was right: although I've been on easier treks with far less fatigue and injury, this climb has somehow been more satisfying than any of them. Long past the short term thrill of the return, I am left with an enduring buzz. This one feels like an achievement.

The border with Zaire is not too far from Kasese, and we reach the crossing with two long bus rides. Being a quiet and isolated post, it's notorious for extracting bribes, and after heavy negotiations we reluctantly relinquish a carton of cigarettes. But once across the border, we soon discover another setback: there are no bus services inside Zaire that reach this far out; instead, we will have to resort to walking and hitching rides whenever we can.

The first small settlement we reach has only basic facilities, and we are lucky to get the last room in a run down hostel. A quick search reveals only one very basic shop and no cooked food, and as we close in on our destination, it is becoming clear that we have a problem: provisions are hard to locate, and there are no more towns en route to offer us accommodation or food. Instead, we will have to stock up on biscuits and bananas, hoping it will see us through the next leg.

We set off early the next day, but after four long hours of walking with packs, we get the uneasy feeling that we are lost. Reliant as we are on passers-by for directions, we are suddenly filled with doubt, but persevere nonetheless up the dirt tracks that wind through the countryside. It is a huge relief then, when we finally spot our objective in the distance. Ahead of us, at the foot of some gently rolling hills, lies the Djomba base hut for expeditions to the Virunga National Park.

This important preservation area for the mountain gorilla has been in decline for the past five years, with poaching becoming a serious threat; they are mainly killed for their meat, with their extremities sold off as trophies or lucky charms: hands for ashtrays, heads as curiosities. But there are still three large families being tracked by the rangers in these parts, and we are hopeful of arranging a trek to see them. Although the cost of these expeditions is not cheap, at a hundred dollars each, all the profits are used for their conservation.

Unfortunately though, it appears that we have arrived at the wrong time. All the hut beds are full, taken up by a Japanese film crew who are stationed here for the next two weeks. We are told by the rangers to come back in three days time when they will try to fit us into their schedule. The delay is disappointment enough, but now we face a more immediate problem; once again we have nowhere to sleep the night ...

After three hours walk through the countryside, we finally locate the Catholic Mission we've been recommended, closer to six miles away than the three that we were told. It seems odd to think that we might be sleeping in a classroom again, but we are pleasantly surprised when instead we are shown to a dormitory. And with proper beds and showers, we are now missing only one important thing - food. Long exhausted of our biscuit supplies, we quickly venture into the surrounding hills to search out new provisions.

But this is rural Africa. For miles around there are only small villages, each with its sprinkling of thatched-roof mud huts and not much else. Between them, the rolling green hills are criss-crossed with a network of small ploughed fields, contrasting each other with their disparate crops. It's a beautiful pastoral scene, but our extensive quest yields very little: three kiwi fruit in one village, two small potatoes in the next. This is all they will reluctantly sell; the produce is for their consumption only. We appear to be stuck in a vast expanse of subsistence farmers.

And so on that first night, and on subsequent days, I experience something new: the extremely unpleasant condition of being close to starvation. The pain is physical as well as psychological; we have been walking hard all day but we have nothing to regenerate our muscles with. And as we watch the two tiny potatoes taking an age to cook on our small camping stove, the smell is like slow torture. When the gas fizzles and dies, and we have no replacement cartridge, the potatoes are devoured half-cooked nevertheless; and all they do is leave us wanting more ...

On the third day, we are allowed to join an expedition as promised; there will be eight of us in all, including the ranger and his assistant. The group of gorillas we are going to visit has already been accustomed to human presence, and we need only track them down. These groups usually move two or three miles each day while foraging from tree to tree, and our ranger soon picks up the trail from where they were last spotted. After an hour we are upon them - a few black shapes in the trees ahead - and we tread carefully as we approach.

We have been rehearsed already in how to behave in front of these powerful animals. They are strong enough to tear you limb from limb, but aggression can be averted if you adopt a submissive pose. This involves crouching down and casting your eyes downwards. It doesn't sound a particularly instinctive reaction, and I wonder how easy it will be to enact should an emergency arise. Soon enough, I find out.

At first we stand on the fringes of the group in quiet observation, but after several minutes of checking us out, the silverback decides to assert his authority. From twenty feet away he pounds his chest and charges straight at us. I crouch down quickly as instructed, and before I can register what's happening, he comes to a sudden halt only four feet away. He stares at me for an eternity, then finally relaxes. We appear to have passed the test.

After that we are able to get closer to the animals. It's a large group of about fourteen gorillas, including a newborn baby that measures barely twelve inches. They play and eat lazily around us as if we are not there. Later, one of the larger females bumps into me in passing. Something of little significance to her has a huge impact on me; to feel part of their world, to be accepted like this, even if only for an hour, is a humbling experience. The trust they exhibit shows a wonderful yet dangerous innocence; it only serves to remind us of the responsibility we have to preserve these magnificent beasts.

Although our hunger has been little sated over the last few days, the gorilla expedition was well worth the excruciating wait. And now we can head to the nearest market town about twenty miles away, where sustenance awaits us. Despite its proximity, it takes half a day to reach, with rides that do not go much faster than walking pace on the muddy and broken roads; but when we finally arrive, we gorge on all the fruit there is to offer.

And as we head further south through Zaire, our progress remains just as sluggish. A typical ride is on a pick up truck laden with more people and possessions than you would think physically possible. A mountain of rice sacks, chicken cages, pots and pans, is topped by ten or twelve passengers. We perch precariously on the edge of this mound with our legs dangling over the sides, as the truck bounces heavily along the dirt road. It's an endurance test mainly concentrated on the buttocks. Every now and then though, relief is at hand, when one of the wheels becomes stuck in the mud, and we all dismount for a collective push. These long and painful journeys eventually take us to Goma, on the north shore of Lake Kivu, where we quickly find our rewards - a shop that sells French baguettes and cheese, a rare luxury in Africa, and an assortment of lively bars for us to drink beer in the evenings. The intention is to take the boat service from here to Bukavu on the south side of the lake; however, we soon discover that it's no longer operational, and another long road trip beckons for our sore backsides.

So far we have been skirting Rwanda on our journey south due to the civil unrest there, but we are now heading to a country that is similar both in size and tribal composition - Burundi. Its capital, Bujumbura, is the starting point for the boat trip we plan to take along Lake Tanganyika, and we are told on arrival that the next service is in four days time.

We decide to spend our wait here in a guest house that's famous amongst travellers. On the outskirts of the city an American couple continually open their doors to passing travellers, offering both food and lodging free of charge. The only request from them is that you say grace before meals and attend church on Sundays. Although Neil and I are far from religious, we are both curious and frugal enough to embrace such an opportunity. The elderly couple turn out to be eccentric and charming, and the food they serve is excellent. Over breakfast they offer insight into the country's problems; we are told that tensions are high between the two main tribes, the ruling Tutsis and the Hutus, after a massacre in the north a few years ago. It's the reverse of the situation in Rwanda where the Hutus are in power, but exactly the same kind of ethnic cleansing. They fear of an eruption of violence in this country on a scale not seen since the seventies. In fact, it would be only two more years before their prediction came true ...

The ship, when it arrives, is called the MV Liemba and is something of a legend. Used as a warship by the Germans in the first world war, it has been running the length of Africa's longest lake for several decades, after being scuttled and raised again in the twenties. On board, it's comfortable enough; we travel second class sleeping in bunks, and there are enough locals cooking food on the decks for us to eat well along the way.

At Kigoma though, I bid farewell to Neil. He is heading to Zambia and Namibia, and I through Tanzania back to Kenya, where I will soon be reunited with Jamila and Otto. He has promised to join me in six weeks time in Watamu, when we plan to fly to India for the last leg of our journey. It seems like a reasonable plan. Unbeknown to me, however, it will be the last time that I set eyes on him ....

20. india

The intrusion of those plain clothes CID into my peaceful life in Watamu has woken me from my reverie. My simple existence here has been coasting for several weeks, and although Otto's progress is reward enough, a decision is beckoning nevertheless.

Neil has not contacted me since I returned to Watamu, except to say that he was heading to Luderitz on the Namibian coast to dive for diamonds commercially. It's a dangerous job that pays well, and it seems likely he will be stuck there for a while. At the same time my Kenyan visa needs extending soon, so I must either leave now, or prolong the indecision for another four weeks. Jamila, however, puts most of the burden on me:

"Whatever you decide, I will do. If you go to India, I will wait," she says, with a calmness that belies the futility of her situation. Neither of us are in any doubt as to the fragility of our relationship. Without sufficient finances I cannot stay long in Kenya, and the fantasy of starting a business here has quickly been laid to rest. Conversely, Jamila has no chance of entering the UK. Not even marriage would be enough - the ability to support your spouse financially is one of the main visa stipulations, and I am without a house or a job. The solution then can only lie in my return to the UK. But before I can even think about that, I first need to finish what I have already started ...

India is in some ways the missing piece from my travelling portfolio. Although I do not consciously collect countries like trophies, it is, however, the most talked about place to travel in the world, and for many travellers it is also their first. For some reason it has had less appeal to me in the past; perhaps because I like my beer too much, or perhaps because the hardships of travel there are so commonly recounted. But with my travelling legs now weary and Bombay only a short hop away, this feels like my last chance to visit.

My arrival on Indian soil is at once both exhilarating and foreboding. The plane skims the roofs of the nearby slums as it lands precariously on a runway lined with the shelters of the poor and the destitute. They seem to be spilling onto the tarmac from all sides; it's an appropriate welcome to a subcontinent renowned for its widespread poverty.

But downtown Bombay is a different story. The buildings are modern and smart, the parks green, and the colourful streets lit up by bright red buses and yellow-black taxis. In a hostel there, tucked away in a back street, I resolve to make plans for my next move. Unfortunately I have arrived in the heat of the summer when the temperatures on the plains are regularly in their forties, and it seems wise to head north to the hills where the climate will be more tolerable. An English couple next door, far better prepared than me, are heading north to Rajastan with an itinerary mapped out for the next three months. After some discussion, they allow me to tag along.

Simon and Jude are from Chelmsford, and bring with them a laid-back attitude and an easy going charm. Travelling by train with them in a group is not only companionable, it also makes life far easier, as we share the burden of queuing for tickets and fighting off touts in the streets and concourses along the way. The trains are slow and ponderous, and food and drink is supplied to us regularly at every stop through the open windows - 'chai', a sickly sweet tea in disposable clay cups, and freshly made bhajis and samosas to eat. Nevertheless, the heat and the crowded carriages make the journey exhausting, and we arrive at our destination desperate for a shower and a bed.

The place we have chosen to stay turns out to be astounding value. For less than a dollar a night, my room has an all-important fan and opens out onto the beautiful Lake Pichola in Udaipur. It's here where the magical Lake Palace, now a five star hotel, sits on an island reached only by motor launch. On a hill overlooking the lake and hotel is the equally majestic City Palace. This is one of the most romantic towns of Rajastan, and a favourite for honeymooners the world over. And as we eat our dinner on a rooftop restaurant with the sun going down over the hills, I face for the first time the most difficult dilemma that India will throw at me. At double the cost of my room, it's a huge extravagance, but the setting we are in makes it irresistible. Quickly giving in to temptation, I order my first refreshingly cold Kingfisher beer ...

The following days we spend touring the palaces, wandering the streets and soaking up the atmosphere. Away from its picturesque lakeside, Udaipur is like any other Indian town - busy, noisy and sprawling - and the hawkers and touts that constantly intrude on us are difficult to tolerate. It is, perhaps, the least endearing aspect of India. But our next stop has been chosen for being less touristic, and should be somewhat quieter; after five days in Udaipur, we are heading for the hill station of Mount Abu.

Hill stations are particularly popular in the summer, when the cooler air is sought out by Indian families on vacation. There are several of these dotting the plains of India, a hangup from the colonial days when the British escaped the heat to drink their tea and eat their scones. This particular one even has a polo field, and sits on a plateau at over a thousand metres, allowing a temperature drop of nearly ten degrees.

The town appears to be full of newly marrieds and their wedding parties, who arrive in white Ambassador cars bedecked with flowers and ribbons, then venture out on boats into the middle of the lake. At dusk, the crowds flock to a nearby hill to watch the sunset; it's a busy and sociable event, with all kinds of street sellers offering food and refreshments to the picnicking families. Curiously, we are the only Westerners there.

And in this cooler air we decide to try out the local whisky. As an alternative to beer, it is far cheaper, yet comes with a considerable risk. There have been large fatalities reported in the local press, when the occasional batch of branded whisky has been improperly distilled; the unfortunate drinkers have died of alcohol poisoning. With that in mind, we choose a more expensive label from the dozens on offer, and drink tentatively at first. The taste is as close to industrial alcohol as I can imagine, but we persevere nonetheless, and the evening is a welcome relief from the last few weeks of sobriety. The conclusion the next morning, however, is unequivocal; a severe migraine and a lingering taste of ethanol in the back of the throat is a constant and nauseous reminder of the night before. It's the last time we will experiment with the hard stuff here ...

But as we set off for the next town, Pushkar, I realise there is an aspect to India that I am enjoying immensely - the cuisine. Although it is often reported as being inferior to the typical fare from an Indian restaurant in England, the food here is tasty and varied; eating curry twice a day is a real pleasure compared to the bland food I've been accustomed to in Africa. The restaurants I most often frequent serve Thalis, a tray containing several dishes at once, which is topped up regularly by roaming waiters armed with giant pots; the food is always consumed with the fingers, and there is no choice but to follow suit. Regional differences mean there is always something new to encounter as we move from town to town, with some states more vegetarian than others. And the food, like the accommodation, is dirt cheap; if you can avoid beer, your money will last twice as long as in Africa, perhaps a key reason for India's popularity amongst the young and the budget minded.

Pushkar is a Mecca of sorts for just this type of traveller. Set by a lake with its beautiful white domed architecture lining the shore, it resembles Udaipur, but on a smaller, quieter scale; it's the place that you come to escape the crazed pace and hustle of the cities. There are shops here that legally sell bhang, a cannabis preparation traditionally used for cultural and spiritual reasons, and which is made into lassi drinks of varying strength and served in many of the restaurants. For all these reasons perhaps, this town has in the past been a haven for that long endangered species, the hippy. And it is here that I meet for the first time what appears to be the newest encapsulation of this phenomenon; young females, usually the offspring of affluent families, going native by wearing saris and sporting red dots, or bindis, on their foreheads. It's unclear if the religious significance of the bindi is understood by them, but I'm not in the slightest bit interested in finding out.

And it's not long before I decide to move on quickly from this place. Unfortunately Jude has become sick with food poisoning, an inevitable consequence of our frugal existence, and although Simon and I suffered briefly with the same affliction, she has since deteriorated and needs to rest up for several days. So I am heading north alone, aiming for the cool air of the Himalayas, with the hope of running into them again somewhere.

There are, however, many things to see along the way; in the pink-walled city of Jaipur in Rajastan, I feel a strange commitment to visit every single one of its many forts and maharaja palaces. It's true that each is impressive by itself, especially the observatory, but for me they soon become repetitive, and I am afforded much less privacy now that I am travelling alone. On one such tour of the Nahargahr fort I am accosted by an Indian tourist offering me a banana. He responds to my polite refusal of the fruit by grabbing my wrist, and a struggle ensues that's hard to make sense of. To resolve the situation, I grab the banana and throw it over the wall of the battlements. This is, of course, the most amusing thing he's seen all day, and the man subsequently follows me around the castle, no doubt in expectation of more light entertainment. The experience is unsettling and not uncommon; there is a cultural difference here in which personal space is rarely respected, and it's hard to know how to react when it's invaded. I have, however, learnt of a good response when cornered by one the many touts for business. Whenever they ask you a question:

"Sahib! Sahib! You need taxi? You need hotel? Very cheap price. You come with me Sahib," you simply reply:

"If not, but maybe."

Apart from the fun of seeing that bewildered look on their face, it usually confuses them long enough to allow you a quick exit ...

The last thing for me to do in Jaipur is to sample that well known staple of Indian culture, the Bollywood film. The Raj Mandir theatre is one of the most ornate cinemas in the world, and is worth a visit for this reason alone; decorated in art deco style with chandeliers and glittering mosaics, it resembles the interior of a fairy tale palace. The film I have come to watch is a four hour long marathon that charts the love story of a handsome young couple; when they are not breaking out into song and dance with the whole cast, the plot contains drama, action, intrigue and a slow motion tennis match between two scantily clad girls. It's probably the closest I've been to understanding Indian culture since I've been here.

On the way to Agra from Jaipur, I decide to stop at the Ranthambore tiger reserve. The centre for tours is based at an old maharaja hunting lodge that has since become a hotel, but still retains the old black and white photos of its previous inhabitants on the walls. In these pictures, the shooting parties stand proudly in Victorian poses, with the dead tiger spoils on parade at their feet. It's an ominous sign. After a days safari by jeep, where the closest we get to seeing a tiger is a footprint in the mud, we are told the reason why; only weeks earlier, the observation huts were rented out by a gang of poachers who shot dead six tigers in one night as they drank at a watering hole. The population stood at less than thirty tigers before the incident; it's hard to see how they will survive for much longer.

The Taj Mahal on the contrary, does not disappoint. I had been advised to visit it in the different light of dawn and dusk, so I find a place to stay nearby. With fewer visitors at those times, the site is also at its most serene, and it's enough just to sit in quiet contemplation in the gardens. Like the pyramids, the ambition of this endeavour is impressive, but this time in the detail rather than the size; every inch of its surface is covered with intricate patterns etched into the marble and inlaid with semi-precious stones, the designs and craftsmanship sourced from all over the seventeenth century world. As a monument to love built by a Moghul Emperor in memory of his dead wife, it's a folly of sorts, but an accomplished one nonetheless.

I stop briefly in Delhi, where I find a letter from Jamila awaiting me in the Poste Restante: Otto is improving, and has been seen by a doctor who thinks he may have a mild form of autism rather than downs syndrome. It's a positive letter. But there is still no news from Neil, and I have to assume now that he will not be joining me in India. It's a disappointment for me; we had planned to buy Enfield motorcycles and tour the country on them, and I've yet to find anyone here to take his place. Nevertheless, the news has strengthened my resolve; without much hesitation, I get on a train and head north for the hills.

Dharamsala is the home to the Dalai Lama, who has been exiled here since 1959 after the Chinese invasion of Tibet. Scattered around the hillsides in nearby McLeod Ganj are the colourful prayer flags and stones placed by the residents of the nearby monasteries, and the ambience here is as tranquil as the Buddhists themselves. The main street is lined with small businesses offering palmistry and meditation courses, books on spiritualism, and authentic Tibetan food. Lying in the foothills of the Himalayas, the temperature is now in the comfortable twenties, and the air is cool and clear. The area has a number of scenic walks, and it's refreshing to be able to wander around with complete freedom and without interference. After a week of blissful relaxation, I wonder why I took so long in coming here. It feels like a turning point in my journey.

Just east of Dharamsala, with a similar elevation and climate, lies Manali, the first stop on a circular route that I am planning to take through the Himalayas. It's another popular and picturesque hill station, but it's also famous for the quality of its cannabis crop. On the bus there I make friends with a Danish traveller, and we decide to sample the local produce together. We venture into the surrounding villages where many of the hippies hangout, and amongst the rustic timber buildings we eventually find a dealer. Rather unwisely I allow my new acquaintance to roll the joint, and later suffer the consequences in my hotel room. The delayed effect of cannabis means that, unlike alcohol, it's easy to imbibe too much before you realise it, and this particular joint was far too strong. As it hits me wave after wave, I am seized by a panic attack focused entirely on my heavily beating heart; it seems ready to explode, and my increasing paranoia only makes it faster and louder. To tear my mind away from these thoughts, I stand under a cold shower for what feels like an eternity; the distraction of this stream of water beating constantly on my head serves its purpose well, but only after a couple of hours do the effects recede and I feel safe enough to leave the confines of the bathroom. The Dane next door must no doubt have been wondering what I've been doing. When I finally emerge, I tell him: I've just beaten my previous record for the longest shower ...

The next leg takes me on one of the highest roads in the world. Early in the journey the bus is delayed by a truck being winched upside down from a deep ravine; lying next to a glacier whose melting waters are flowing fast across the road, it's not hard to work out what happened: this road has only just become passable, and the driver was perhaps a little too impatient. Trucks like this are a constant menace on these winding roads, but I console myself with the fact that the driver of our bus seems cautious enough. We continue up the mountain pass at a slow and steady pace until we finally reach the top after ten hours of driving; on the brow of the hill, a sign written in typical Indian fashion reads:

'You Are Passing Through Second Highest Pass Of The World. Taglangla. Height 17582 Feet.

Unbelievable Is It Not?'

The passengers get out for a quick refreshment stop, but I nervously await our departure. I have heard recently of a bus being stranded up here overnight, with its occupants quickly succumbing to altitude sickness; although it doesn't feel like it, this bus is now at a height equivalent to the summit of Mont Blanc or the Mount Everest base camp.

We eventually arrive in Leh after dark, and it's not until the following day that I can survey the magical world that I have arrived in. The region of Ladakh is an extension of the Tibetan plateau, and its resemblance to Tibet is more than just geographical. Many of the inhabitants are Tibetan, and their culture and architecture permeates the region. Red-white monasteries and temples perch on small rocky hilltops overlooking lush green valleys; this intricate mesh of fields, fed by the melting glaciers, is bordered sharply by tall barren mountains streaked with purples, browns and greys. It's a beautiful contrast of colours, and one that can only be seen in the summer months when the snow has melted and the passes are accessible.

Like their surroundings, the people too are colourful and quiet. I watch as a large crowd gathers to witness a polo match; like the hill tribes of northern Thailand, it's mainly the women who dress in traditional clothes: black robes, top hats, pink scarves, coloured beads and pony tails; apart from the scarlet-robed monks, the men and children dress in an eclectic mix of western clothes, like the rich pickings of a church jumble sale.

I decide to go on an organised trek to the nearby mountains, and on the first day I make friends with two solo travellers like myself, Pete and Hannah. From the U.S. and Belgium respectively, they are an odd pairing who at first glance appear to have swapped sexes: Pete, camp and fragile with long curly hair, and Hannah, stoic and stocky with an army-style crew cut. The three of us make an interesting dynamic as we climb to altitudes none of us has experienced before. Ascending a pass at twenty-thousand feet, every step requires a rest and a large intake of breath before switching to the next leg; I feel like a grossly overweight man trying to climb the stairs. Strangely though, even at these giddy heights, we barely reach the snow-line.

After the trek, the three of us decide to explore the Indus Valley together. Lit every day by clear blue skies, this dramatic environment is without doubt the most beautiful I've seen on all my travels. We stop at the Buddhist Gompas along the way, exploring the countryside by day, and staying every night in the guest rooms of the monasteries. And after many days of friendly persuasion in these tranquil surroundings, I finally convince my two fellow travellers to join me on the next leg of my journey. Though a dangerous place to visit, we will carry on down this highway all the way to Kashmir ...

The capital Srinagar is at present the centre of an uprising by Kashmiri insurgents, who are demanding independence from India. The Indian army are there in force, as tensions also build with Pakistan over a long standing border dispute. Tourists have been advised not to travel there, but my argument to Pete and Hannah is that this will make the region both cheaper and more rewarding.

In fact the journey itself is reason enough to go. The two hundred and sixty mile road takes two days to navigate, as it winds up and down the mountains of the Himalayas with spectacular views all the way. A long stretch in the middle is one way only, changing direction at noon to allow the long convoys of lorries to pass each other. We manage to get a ride on one such truck, sitting high above the cabin in an open luggage box, but we have concerns about the sobriety of our driver after spotting a half-drunk bottle of whisky in his cab. As the truck snakes around the hairpin bends, the views looking down the ravines are dizzying, and I mentally prepare myself to jump off at the first sign of any listing. Meanwhile, the road signs reinforce our anxiety with their witticisms:

'Be Soft On My Curves'

'Be Mr Late, Better Than Late Mr'

'If You Sleep, Your Family Will Weep'

But the most apt for our situation appears later on, while approaching a particularly hairy bend in the road:

'After Whisky, Driving Is Risky'

After an overnight stop in Kargil, we zigzag down a precipitous pass that marks the beginning of the Kashmir Valley. In a clear delineation of environments, we descend from the elevated and arid Tibetan Plateau into the rain clouds below. Suddenly the landscape resembles Switzerland, with thick banks of conifers now clinging to the steep mountain slopes, and meadows filled with wild flowers. Because of our concerns about Srinagar, we decide to disembark at Sonamarg where we can by-pass the capital and enjoy a four day trek to Pahalgam instead. The altitude now is manageable, and the easy walk takes us over a glacial mountain range, with our guide's ponies taking the strain of both our backpacks and a large circular tent for us to sleep in. At the halfway point, however, we all succumb to a dose of giardia almost simultaneously; distinguishable from other gut infections by its stomach cramps, sulphurous burps and bright yellow diarrhoea, it becomes a hot topic of conversation along the way. However, it's a small inconvenience alongside the pleasure of walking unburdened amongst the valleys and hills of Kashmir.

Pahalgam, a pretty hill station village, is deserted when we arrive, with only a handful of travellers staying in the many hotels. We choose the most popular, a Swiss-like chalet on the bank of a river rapids, where we hole up for a few days. The atmosphere is friendly and conspiratorial, and there are favourable reports of Srinagar from our fellow guests; safety is apparently less of an issue than we imagined. I decide at once to travel onwards there, but despite my best efforts at persuasion, Pete and Hannah remain steadfast. This time they will not be joining me ...

A stay on one of the elaborate houseboats on Dal Lake is a requisite for any visitor to the region. Built during the Raj by the British, who were prevented from owning land, there are hundreds of these moored permanently on the south side of the lake, each a small piece of England locked in a time warp from the nineteen thirties. Because of the conflict they are largely empty and abandoned, but I team up with a middle-aged Frenchman who arrived with me on the bus to negotiate our stay with one of the owners; the deal we finally agree on gives us full board for less than a pound. It turns out that Pierre has a great life story, and an immensely entertaining way of telling it. He worked for many years in Paris as a hotel porter, before making it rich as a car salesman. His high flying lifestyle had the classic hallmarks - yacht, brand new BMW, gold Rolex watch - and his hobbies of hang-gliding and flying World War Two planes resulted in two near-fatal accidents. But after a messy divorce, he decided to give it all up and travel the world; he is now making his way slowly to Australia, where he plans to use his flying experience to work as a crop duster. To me, who has given up precisely nothing in order to travel, this rags-to-riches-to-rags tale is both humbling and poignant; it seems that despite his success, he has never let it enslave him.

As I venture out from our houseboat, Srinagar appears to be functioning normally despite a huge army presence, and I am able to explore the centre on foot without restraint. It's a busy market town where dilapidated wooden buildings line rivers full of houseboats, and where in true Hindu tradition, cows roam the streets lazy and unattended. But as I turn a corner to head down one of the banks of Dal Lake, I hear loud gunshots coming from nearby. In front of me, hiding behind a car for protection, are four soldiers with guns. One of them beckons me to carry on walking past them:

"It's okay. You can come through. The sniper is far away."

Although temporarily thrown by this apparent contradiction in logic, I continue nevertheless, walking sheep-like to his instructions, as the shots keep echoing around me. It's only in afterthought that I consider why he would need a shield and I wouldn't; perhaps he assumed that a distant sniper would only aim at soldiers and could somehow distinguish between us. Of course, I will never know ...

The overnight train journey back to Delhi is the hardest yet. Pierre and I can only manage to get third class tickets, and the only floor space we can find to sleep on is in second. We ignore the objections from one of the middle class female passengers, and a diatribe follows:

"You people, you come to our country, you have no respect ..."

We are so tired that we live entirely up to her expectations by returning the compliments with interest. By the time we arrive in Delhi, the experience has been so exhausting that we can barely speak. We avoid eye contact, as if each is a reminder to the other of this recent trauma, and part silently, heading our own separate ways ...

Although the train journey seems like a timely reminder that my stay here is almost up, after a few days rest I decide to attempt one last excursion from Delhi. Having stocked up on antibiotics for the giardia, I set off for the mountains once again, but this time to a new country altogether. This small but intriguing nation is within easy reach, and it seems foolish to waste such an opportunity; I am heading for Nepal.

The capital Katmandu has an almost fairy tale reputation amongst travellers, not only as a base for trekking in the Himalayas, but as a vibrant and colourful city in its own right. I choose a room on the top floor of my hotel, allowing views across the city of the many domes and spires of the temples and pagodas. At dusk, the kids assemble on the rooftops to fly their kites, and the sky is awash with colour as they fight one another for control of their territory. But in the day the city is teeming with tourists, and it's hard to spot any solo travellers amongst the crowds. After a few days sightseeing, feeling somewhat alone and lacking in purpose, I decide to book a stay in a nearby Buddhist monastery.

Gazing out over the lush Katmandu valley from the crest of a hill about ten miles out of town is the Kopan monastery. It was made famous recently for discovering the reincarnation of it's founder, Lama Yeshe, in a young Spanish boy born to a student of his; in a test designed to authenticate the claim, the child apparently identified belongings from his earlier life, including a pair of sunglasses. This large complex has been renting out rooms since the seventies to visitors who wish to learn about Buddhism and experience the day to day life of a monk. But there are rules: fornication, drinking, and smoking are all forbidden during my ten day stay. And as a severe nicotine addict, it is the latter that is my biggest challenge.

Although I fall asleep regularly during the somewhat monotonous lectures by the resident Lama, I enjoy the lively discussions afterwards about the ideas behind their religion. It has a well meaning and relatively benign philosophy, although the concept of reincarnation is hard to overcome. Karma is just as contentious for me, as it implies that what happens to you is related to how good you are; my own experience of life suggests something far more haphazard. I ask one of the teachers what in his opinion causes a fatal air crash:

"The plane must have a collectively bad karma," he replies, after some thought.

"What if my karma is good, though?"

"Then you should look carefully at the other passengers."

Queuing up to board a plane will never be the same for me again ...

I return to Delhi from Katmandu and Pokhara without attempting a trek from either of those towns; the two that I have done in Ladakh and Kashmir have been easily sufficient for my lazy soul. I do return as a non-smoker, however, with the attendant health benefits that I have been lacking for nearly fourteen years. And there is still enough energy for a stop in Varanasi, a holy city of ghats and funeral pyres on the banks of the Ganges, where the bodies of the recently deceased can be seen floating by while the locals bathe in the waters nearby.

But after travelling alone for so long now, it feels like I'm just connecting dots on a map; I've spent four months in India now, enough to satisfy my curiosity. And as the train pulls in to Delhi station, where I will soon board my flight back to London, I notice that my bag has been broken into overnight. Missing is the only expensive item that I carry with me - my camera. In fact it is the very same Nikon F2 that I bought from that thieves market in Peru. Perhaps this is just a case of a camera with very bad karma ...

Later, as my plane circles London for what seems like an interminably long thirty minutes, a loud noise makes me wonder if there is something mechanically wrong with the plane. As these irrational thoughts begin to mount, I remember two predictions from the past. At nineteen years old, my palm had been read by the French girlfriend of my busking partner Ben. She had predicted a long journey that ended suddenly when I was twenty-nine:

"I am not sure, I don't mean to worry you, but the ending is sudden. Like a death ..."

And two months ago in Dharamsala I had reluctantly agreed to pay for a reading by a persistent hawker. He had cold read me most of the time, but then said something that caught my attention:

"You will have a big success. Very big."

"When?" I asked.

"Let me see ... when you are twenty-nine, I would say."

"I'm already twenty-nine," I replied, disappointedly.

Although I don't consider myself to be overly superstitious, it's hard to ignore the coincidence of that same number being seen again somewhere in the palm of my hand.

The plane, however, lands without issue. This is the beginning of a new era of congestion at Heathrow; circling London will soon become a frequent occurrence for long haul flights.

And that means that I, thank Buddha, will live to see thirty ....

the pendulum swings

You must be wondering: where have I been?
Why no comment, while this long march through the subcontinents of the world drags onwards?

I have been biding my time, of course, waiting ...

For just as sure as water will find its level, so too will this lost soul soon come home to roost.
For who can ignore for long that powerful tug of the strings that wakes up many a sleeping heart?
Who can walk away so easily when others become dependent on you?

And with that awakening, the weight of the world comes crashing down; that leaden stole of responsibility so long averted is suddenly upon him.
At first it sits loose on the shoulders, then pulls tightly around the neck ...

And what of those worn and weary legs? Has the prophecy of charlatans indeed predicted an end to these nomadic pursuits?
Perhaps. But just as likely, this is life in it's usual random flux: the end of the road is as inevitable as the setting sun; and the coincidence of numbers is everywhere to be found ...

And whether this change of heart and change of direction will be judged to be foolish or wise, opportune or folly, remains to be seen.
The journey, nevertheless, has ended, and the free spirit dulled.
It is the end of an era; the pendulum has swung.

21. betrayal

For the first six weeks in London I hear nothing from Jamila, with three of my letters going unreplied. Then, as we approach Christmas of 1991, one finally arrives through the letterbox. Its contents, though, are disturbing. The letter is rambling and incoherent, but some basic facts are clear: Jamila was arrested in a cafe in Nairobi and has been in jail for the last month. The police in Kenya are regularly locking up illegal immigrants, and an earlier letter from her had described how she had narrowly avoided arrest by bribing the police. The problem is that Jamila left her ID card in a Mombasa night club last year, and has been trying ever since to locate an acquaintance who picked it up. Without an ID card, you are effectively illegal in Kenya. But this is not her explanation for the arrest. Instead she writes:

Jon I think I told you before that I suspect my real father was French according to what I heard a step sister say. Well I discovered recently that my father was a British Saint who was murdered by the Kenyan Govt. So when they saw me praying to Jesus to help me they kidnapped me from a cafe in Nairobi on the first of November. The reason of my coming from Mombasa to Nairobi was to get my ID but I didn't know these people were looking for me to kill me so that I'll never claim my inheritance. Anyway I was tortured with poisonous drugs and injections to kill me and many other things but Jesus saved me from their hands and right now I'm back in Mombasa.

Later on, the letter becomes even more delusional:

Jon I am prophesied in Revelations Chapter 12 in the bible. Otto is going to be King of England, he shall revenge for my father to capture Kenya back to the British. This is why they tried to use witchcraft to destroy me and Otto. Jon my hair is getting silky and my skin lighter. So the world is waiting for us to be revealed. I think you know that a young King shall be born in the Middle East was prophesied. So this King is Otto.

The rest of the letter is fairly normal, but I am well enough acquainted with mental illness to know that something is seriously wrong; an illness of this type could be triggered by stress, perhaps even the drugs that she was administered. It's a frightening letter; I have never heard this kind of talk from her before, and it's completely out of character. What's clear, though, is that she has suffered an enormous shock and needs my help. Perhaps more than anything, Otto needs my help too ...

I touch down in Mombasa on a charter plane, with a cheap return ticket that I managed to secure at the last minute. I haven't been able to contact Jamila in that short space of time, but I have the address of her workplace and plan to surprise her.

In the outskirts of the city, after an hours walk down some dirt roads by the railway tracks, I find the exact place I'm looking for: Wananchi Marine Products Kenya Limited. Standing loosely outside the building is a small group of women on their morning break from filleting fish. I approach one of them asking for Jamila, and wait while she goes to look inside. Shortly afterwards another woman appears, the boss it would seem, and she has some bad news for me: Jamila left only last week. She doesn't work here anymore ...

I return to my hotel devastated; I've now lost the only way I know of contacting her. In the afternoon, after a regenerative sleep, I set about the enormous task of trying to find her. Faced with a city of one million people, it's a daunting prospect, but I have no choice; armed with a photograph of Jamila and Otto, I visit all the old haunts we used to frequent and more - cafes, bars, shops, anywhere she might have been. The air here is hot and humid, and I pound the dusty streets soaked in sweat.

But it's not until the following day that I get a lead; a woman recognises the photo and directs me to a bar just outside of town where she spotted her. I spend three hours waiting there, until the lady in question turns up - it's not Jamila, and not even a good likeness. Sad and disillusioned, I spend my second night in Kenya alone. These long wretched hours of searching and hoping are a slow mental torture; coming so far, being so close, yet still unable to touch ...

On the fourth day I have almost run out of ideas, when a fellow diner in my hotel restaurant gives me a new lead: there was a girl that looked just like Jamila living in the street behind the hotel last week, but he thinks she may have moved out; she even had a son with the same light complexion as Otto. I quickly visit the building in question, and it turns out to be true; Jamila was staying here recently, only a stone's throw from the hotel we occupied whenever we were in Mombasa. She vacated the room last week and has headed up the coast. And now, by instinct, I know exactly where she will be ...

After the three hour matatu ride to Watamu, it doesn't take me long to find out where she's staying. I locate the small African hotel tucked away in one of the alleyways, and knock on her door. The search to find her has been such an odyssey that the suspense for me now is unbearable; when Jamila opens the door and we embrace, it feels like the reunion of a long lost lover, her fresh yet familiar body melting into mine. Otto is there too and welcomes me with a surprised "baba!". It is a moment to savour, and it's several hours before I come down from my high.

The following morning, however, the reality of why I am here sets in; the letter has brought me running to her side, but it's still unclear how I can help. The first thing I attempt to tackle is the delusional aspect of her paranoia, and it soon appears that these beliefs are locked behind an impenetrable shell. When I challenge her logic, the defences come down and there is only silence; rationality is no match for her convictions. And trying to convince her that she is ill and should seek help falls on equally deaf ears. Although she functions normally when not discussing her beliefs, there is no doubt that she has changed; she is colder, and her eyes have a glaze that wasn't there before. Despite the terrible trauma that she suffered, part of me wonders if this side to her was always there, but hidden from view ...

Otto, though, needs help of his own. To that end we go to visit the Children's District Officer in Malindi. The plan is to arrange a formal payment from his biological father for his special education needs. Schooling in Kenya is not free, and Jamila has always squandered the sporadic payments Otto's father has given her. The news, however, is ambivalent; they cannot force him to pay any money, but will nevertheless talk to him on Jamila's behalf. A date is set for this meeting, though it will be after I have returned to London.

Meanwhile, the three of us are happily ensconced in a small hotel on the beach front, with Otto playing with the new toys I brought from England for him. For a few days we enjoy this simple existence which, despite the spectre of Jamila's illness, is relaxed once again. The harmony, however, is short lived. Late one afternoon, two policemen knock on the door of our hotel room. They have come to arrest Jamila ...

On the daily news we are often bombarded with tales of untold cruelty between one human and another; but when it's close to you, as it is this time, the pain sinks so much deeper. Instilled in me now is something quite ugly that I have never had to experience before - pure hatred for another human being. For as we sit in the police station, it has quickly become clear that the man behind this arrest is Otto's father, Heinz. On the desk now in front of us is the Ugandan passport that Heinz bought Jamila five years ago, when trying to smuggle her out of Somalia for an abortion. Although the passport is a fake bought on the black market, it is evidence enough for the police to lock Jamila up as an illegal immigrant. It is also highly likely that he has paid them off; any attempts I make to argue her case or hint at a bribe are met with intransigence; you cannot bribe a policeman that's already been bribed.

And so, later that night, Jamila is locked in a cell at the police station, and I am left to look after Otto alone. The following morning is surreal, as I walk down the sea front towards the police station hand in hand with Otto, a child I have no relation to, yet who is entirely entrusted to me with the blessing of the authorities. Nearby, running a profitable little business taking wealthy tourists sports fishing on his private boat, is his real father, who has just bribed the police to send his mother to jail. It's hard to make any sense of it.

My anger, though, is tempered by more practical considerations, and the second day of Jamila's stay in jail brings a ray of hope. The judge has set a date for her hearing and set out the terms of bail; the cost to release her will be fifty pounds, the equivalent of about a months average wage here. Although I came out to Kenya with my very last pennies, I have just enough funds to afford it. The long bureaucratic process takes the best part of the day, but just before nightfall she is finally released.

We relocate to Mombasa immediately, both to escape the attentions of those corrupt policemen and to search for the elusive ID card that could have saved her from this predicament in the first place. For Jamila, of course, this new turn of events has done nothing to dull her paranoia; if anything this new intervention by the police has reinforced her delusions. For me, however, there is only impotence and despair; I want to fight the cause for Otto more than anyone, but it seems impossible to influence the situation here without money and against a man who appears to be both powerful and nefarious. In many ways I feel that I've made matters worse by coming here, perhaps unwittingly stirring a hornet's nest ...

I leave Jamila the rest of my money before parting, along with strict instructions for her court case which is scheduled four weeks from now; I implore her not to go at all if she cannot retrieve her ID. And after another sad goodbye, I leave for the airport - this time, with so many doubts hanging over our relationship, that I wonder if I will ever be coming back ...

PART 3

22. the knife edge

It's easy for the nerves to get hold of you in a situation like this. As the show gets underway, I can see that there is about an hour in the schedule before our category comes up, and it's impossible to enjoy anything that's going on in the meantime. My breathing is shallow, and my heart starts pounding heavily. What if I have to go up on stage with half a billion people watching? And as my head struggles to contain a body in full panic mode, I slowly begin to realise something. Surely it would be better to win and go through this small inconvenience? Imagine getting so close and losing? There will never be another chance like this.

At once, my body settles down, the heartbeat returns to normal, and I take a long deep breath ...

The year 1992 could easily be seen as a tipping point in my life. One long journey has ended and another about to begin, and right now my world is in the balance, soon to be sent tumbling one way or the other. I am in control of my own destiny, it's true, but only inasmuch as a captain steers a heavy ship through the fog in the vague direction he is going; the details, the destination, nothing is known.

One thing, however, is clear; I have changed. The thought of settling down is no longer anathema to me. Whether it is with Jamila and Otto, or someone as yet unknown, I want to at least be capable of supporting a family.

And as I wait anxiously in London for news of Jamila's court appearance, a feeling of dread sinks in. I had asked her to take a friend with her to court, with a prepaid envelope to convey the news to me should something go wrong. Inexplicably there are no letters forthcoming; a week passes, then two, then three. Instead, a letter from Kurt drops on my doormat once again:

So finally the letter I promised you some weeks ago. But of course I've been kind of busy moving all my gear over to Amsterdam, and somehow managed. Living in a new place makes things more interesting, specially

Amsterdam. Last weekend I found a fridge and a heater both for free (old Chinese saying: he who is patient acquiring things, can spend more money on beer - but you probably know that one already). Pretty hard though living under freezing conditions, I managed to connect the heater, but I'm afraid to use it, getting gassed and all that. Not much trust in myself.

So what about you? Any news from Kenya yet? If any I sure hope it's positive. Any plans of getting over here and see my luxurious apartment, and of course stay a bit longer than previous time. About your asking for a job over here, I think I told you already, money isn't as good as in England, but best chances of getting one (I think) is in April and May when the tourist flow starts. But don't forget Queens Day (30th April) and the 5th May Liberation Day, some really good party days!

Things look kinda bright over here, but also not so nice things happening. The guy I worked with for a year in this second-hand business, Gerard, I think you met him in this bar one night (American), jumped off his apartment 4th floor but somehow survived and is in intensive care, but according to the doctors he is going to make it, although he needs some 2 years to recover (not to mention the psycho bit). Another friend just got convicted for slicing up somebody, but I still have to find out about his sentence. Anyway enough of all the not so nice things in life, but still a part of it. Anyway I really would like you to come over and stay a while, so let me know now what you're up to,
Kurt

Of course I am up to nothing, bar the waiting; I can get post forwarded to me with any news of Jamila, and this seems like the perfect opportunity to see what Amsterdam has to offer. Only a few days later, I book the 'magic bus' to Amsterdam ...

Kurt's new apartment is in a perfect location close to the city centre, in a typical street of quaint narrow houses backing onto one of the many canals. The house has four small flats, one on each floor, and each has it's own attic room on the fifth floor for storage. It is in one of these small rooms that I decide to sleep, rather than intrude on Kurt's privacy. There is one tiny window looking out onto the canal, and the walls are covered with egg cartons from its previous incarnation as a music rehearsal room. Since Kurt's flat is three steep flights of stairs down, I use a large tin lined with disinfectant as an ad-hoc toilet for those middle of the night emergencies. I am no Anne Frank and there is no diary, but it's a similar arrangement. In the second week, I stumble across an abandoned bicycle in the street with one of it's wheels buckled. After buying a handful of new spokes, I manage to fix the wheel, then spray paint the frame Ferrari red to make it my own. A bicycle is one of the best modes of transport to navigate this city's narrow streets and bridges; I am now all set.

Finding a job, however, proves more difficult. Armed with my Dutch phrasebook, I am making some progress with the language, but not nearly enough to negotiate a job interview. Instead, I pursue some English speaking connections to look for building work, but without a skill or a trade, that eventually proves fruitless too. It's not too long before my funds run out, and I find myself in the uncomfortable position of relying on Kurt for sustenance and beer. But just as I'm contemplating defeat, I get the inevitable reprieve: a temp agency that I registered with early on calls to offer me a posting; I am expected at work the very next day at a Nissan processing plant in the western port of the city ...

My commute is a long way by bicycle, but I make it in about forty-five minutes. The plant takes cars off newly arrived cargo ships from Japan and cleans them in a production line in preparation for their delivery to showrooms. My task is to drive the cleaned-up cars off the end of a conveyor and park them outside about fifty yards away, ready to be driven somewhere else by another gang. The job is repetitive and draining, but it feels good to be able to pay my way at last.

And life once more settles into a routine, with workmanlike weekdays and idle weekends to explore my new city. As Kurt promised in his letter, Queens day proves to be one of the best times to see Amsterdam. It's the one day of the year when the laws are relaxed for buying and selling goods; the streets are closed to traffic, and instead they are filled with improvised stalls selling beer and food alongside its residents unwanted possessions, like a city wide jumble sale. At night we cycle the atmospheric streets, thick with smoke from the bonfires lit on every corner, like a city in the grips of an anarchic revolution.

When spring blossoms into summer, the city becomes a playground for further outdoor pursuits: we drink in the parks, listen to free concerts, play competitive mini golf and go sailing with friends. But it's not long before this easy life is interrupted. A problem is developing for me at work, in the form of a colleague suffering from delusions of grandeur. As the longest serving employee in our gang, a twenty something English girl has decided to take matters into her own hands and guide me with her matronly advice several times a day:

"You're parking the cars too close to the lines. They should be three inches to the right."

"Fuck off, you're not my boss," I say politely.

"If you don't do it properly, I'll report you."

"Go ahead," I offer.

Unfortunately, nothing will deflect her from her quest; this small pond that makes her feel so big is way too important to her. No matter what I try, I can't get rid of her.

And then one day, after yet another provocation, I lose it. The cars inside the warehouse are no longer gently driven off, but revved until the wheels spin and smoke belches out of their exhausts; they speed crazily out of the door before screeching to a halt exactly three inches from the line. One of the Japanese supervisors looks bewildered. The next day I am asked not to return to work; it's the first time in my life that I've been sacked.

Although my stay in Amsterdam has lasted barely three months, I leave optimistically with plans afoot. Kurt and I have discussed the idea of starting an introduction agency between East and West Europeans by advertising in Loot, a free-ad newspaper that circulates in Europe. An exploratory trip to Prague by Kurt is imminent. The agency would of course be called Czech-mate.

Meanwhile, as I ponder my next move in London, a letter from Jamila finally arrives in July, four months after her court date. It's a brief but distressing note: she has been in prison for three months, then deported to Uganda, where she's staying now with her step mother. Subsequent letters over the next four weeks allow me to piece together what happened. She fell sick with malaria the day before the court appearance and couldn't attend; she was arrested in her room and taken for psychiatric evaluation before finally being sent to prison. Fortunately, Otto was in the hands of some Somali friends for this whole period. In one of these letters, there is another rambling account of her mysterious white father, a tale mixed with black magic and conspiracy theories similar to before - her illness does not appear to have abated. I write back, this time imploring her to stay in Uganda; I have no idea how to help, I just want her to remain as far away as possible from the Kenyan police ...

To keep going, I get my old job back at the furniture company. The pay is not so good this time - a recession is on it's way, and they have managed to source cheaper labour - but it's money nonetheless. At the same time, I examine all my options. A number of ideas come and go over the months: the Czech-mate business, a washable tattoo business, writing a travel book (Around The World in 80 Cautionary Tales), playing the drums in Spain (where my ex-busking partner Ben now has a band). I even consider applying for a job with my ten-year-old degree, and decide to give it a whirl. Borrowing a suit from Marks and Spencer - fully paid for, then returned for a refund the next day - I travel up to Basingstoke for an interview with a software company. The manager tells me that he enjoyed reading my 'creative' CV (which makes a bold attempt to show how the past eight years of travelling has made me eminently employable), but offers me advice instead of a job. He suggests I get training in something more specific, more vocational. Although I am eager to get working, it seems at least worth a look ...

I find the book quite by chance on the computer science shelf of the University of Kingston library. It has a picture on the front that intrigues me; a music room from a Vermeer painting with harpsichord, table, chair and a checkerboard floor. And inside, more pretty pictures, all of them it turns out, generated by computers. I read a bit of the text. Most of it involves A-level style maths such as vectors, matrices and the physics of light, all quite straightforward for me. But I quickly realise there's something here that I've never seen before in a subject, apart from perhaps architecture: the mergence of art and science into one very practical application, in this case computer graphics.

In fact, I have come to the library to find out about this subject more than any other. A brochure I picked up at the job centre has a scheme for retraining graduates on various high technology courses, and this one in particular has caught my eye. The scheme is generous: tuition fees are free, and students get an allowance that's equivalent to being on the dole; the cost of any rental accommodation is similarly covered by the council. Significantly, the last three months of the ten month course requires a work placement in a company of your choosing, gaining valuable experience. It's an opportunity that comes with no investment or risk, apart from my time. And if a subject could ever be said to be tailor made for me, this one seems to fit like an Armani suit ...

23. a fresh start

After a short and lacklustre interview at Middlesex University where the course will be held, I write a lengthy begging letter to the Dean, fiercely determined not to miss the opportunity. Somehow the campus in North London has impressed me as much as the idea of drawing pretty pictures on a computer; it's a modern looking building, painted in bold primary colours, whose exposed pipework and venting is reminiscent of the Pompidou Centre in Paris. I feel instantly at home. And to add weight to my conviction, I discover that the book that so intrigued me in the library is the exact text for the course.

Two anxious weeks later, the news comes back. Whether by virtue of my letter or not, I have been accepted on the scheme and will start in October ...

It's odd that I find myself back in education. Something that I was so glad to see the back of eight years ago, I now embrace wholeheartedly. The anxieties of that earlier existence still visit me in my dreams - often I awake in the night with a jolt, having opened an exam paper on which every question is gibberish; the dream is a hangup from my Oxford finals, when a lack of preparation forced me to hand in blank sheets of paper for three of my seven exams. But this is somehow different. Where before I lacked a purpose or a goal, here there is a clear chain of events that leads to a job or career of some sort. And this time I am older, more mature, more committed. This course is not just a new chapter, it's a new book, a completely fresh start.

And of course computers have undergone something of a revolution since I left Oxford. Unless you studied Computer Science, there were none to be seen at all on that campus in the early eighties, and the very idea of them was abhorrent to me back then. Now, however, the PC is making its way into homes as well as offices, and is beginning to be seen as a creative as well as a business tool. At the Middlesex campus, we have access to PCs for a couple of hours at the end of each day when we can put our coursework into practice. My initiation, though, is harsh. I've never touched a computer before and have a hard time locating which key to press on the keyboard; a colleague comes to my aid after I scream out in exasperation:

"Where's the 'q'? I can't find the fucking 'q'! How do I quit this fucking program?"

At least a week of frustration ensues, but somehow, like all the fears I had of returning to education, it all calms down. The course itself is not too difficult, and after a few weeks I've written my first program on a PC: a simple perspective cube that spins around randomly, and which the user must then bring to rest with three rotational controls, like unravelling a Rubik's cube. Simple as it sounds, it has a staggering effect on my confidence. I had in fact been wondering if all that grass smoking in Thailand would have addled my grey cells beyond repair; it appears not.

And it's not long before I realise that I have discovered something rare: a craft that I can do, that I enjoy doing, and that according to the proponents of this course, is in demand. Ever keen to escape the pigeonholing of my early education, I now see my foundation in maths as a springboard for more artistic aspirations. It is of course acutely serendipitous; in my long abstention from the rat race, the proliferation of computer applications has only recently begun.

The course has brought together a mixed bag of students from disparate backgrounds, including architects and BBC editors, and a small group of us quickly find common ground. We organise a five-a-side football game, and a 'big night out' every Friday, which sometimes involves entertainment, but which always involves drinking beer; it's very much a student lifestyle, but with most of us having both savings and an allowance, we are far more moneyed this time.

At Christmas I take up another invitation to Amsterdam from Kurt, only this time Stacey joins us later on for the new year celebrations. We smoke and drink and wander amongst the frozen canals in a kind of nostalgic haze. Our time in Sydney is recalled now as something distant and unattainable:

"The two of you were amazing together," she confides in me. "It was like I was in love with both of you ... as one, if you see what I mean ..."

She ends with a typically short, nervous giggle to temper the sentimentality. It is, of course, what I already knew, but the words seem to reflect someone else now, someone from a different time.

When looking to the future though, the talk amongst us is largely apprehensive. Stacey's marriage isn't working out, and neither is Kurt's girlfriend; it feels like all three of us are losing our grip on our relationships simultaneously. But there is hope in the air, as a new year always promises, and we part ways in good spirits ...

In fact the new year does bring me respite in the form of a new romance. Bella is a Londoner of Jamaican origin, introduced to me by a mutual friend; he warns me not to get involved with her, but impulsive as I am, I ignore his advice. She comes with complications: a four year old daughter, a depressive ex-boyfriend who shares custody, and a recent history of drug addiction. But with a vivacious and cheeky persona, and a svelte-like figure so reminiscent of Jamila, I am soon besotted. Friends and family can immediately see how poorly we are suited, but I am blind to those kinds of practical considerations; this is something I desperately need and refuse to relinquish.

Meanwhile Jamila's letters keep coming, and the latest provides me with further anguish. Against my advice, she crossed back into Kenya last year and has been held in a psychiatric hospital for a month. But thinking that I'm in love with someone else now, I no longer feel the same sense of duty that I once felt. Although it's a relief to be able to let go, I'm still left with the overriding sadness and helplessness of it all ...

24. soho

When I enter the office reception in a small back street of Covent Garden and sit down to await my appointment, I am immediately captivated. A reel is playing on a TV monitor, repeating every two or three minutes, showcasing the company's work. It's a mixture of TV idents, title sequences, commercials and music videos. All of it is the result of the image processing and 3D graphics produced by this small company. It's a completely new world to me, and it seems exciting and new.

I am shown around by a very genial girl who introduces me to the staff as well as the computers, all of which seem to have names: Picasso, Rembrandt, Goya and Monet are the Silicon Graphics machines that generate the 3D, Harry the black box that does the final mix. I have been invited for an interview after cold-calling the company with a request to do my placement here. It's not a hard decision for them to make; I don't need a salary, and they happen to have a spare seat in front of one of their older computers. Similar to the expensive Silicon Graphics machine we have at the university, I will be able to work on this one all day instead of the few hours a week I have been limited to before. My course requires a project to be finished by the summer, and I have chosen to write a program that creates 3D trees that can grow from shoots in a similar way to time-lapse photography.

Over the next few months, the company helps me with my project while I work on a few paying jobs as well. I animate pound notes falling down the screen for a BBC documentary on finance, then a floating hot air balloon for an insurance company commercial. But at the same time as this good fortune has come along, my personal life is dealt a crushing blow: Bella decides to end our relationship for reasons that are unfathomable to me. Although it has been short-lived, in my eyes it was still full of promise. It feels like my guts have been ripped out. And she misses, by a few weeks, my breaking news:

"You know, now that Rick's left for the States, we have a vacancy?" says the genial girl, on behalf of the small animation team. "Well, we think you should be the replacement. We just need to convince Phil. We're going to talk to him in the pub tonight."

Phil is the boss, a boozy ex-editor, and he doesn't take long to convince. It turns out that I've secured a job before my course has even ended ...

My first salary negotiations don't go entirely according to plan; I set my heart on a typical graduate starting salary, but instead am offered only half of that. Less than my wage as a delivery driver, it's barely enough to get by on, but I do get one concession - a review in two months. And I am on the move in more ways than one. The same friend I shared with in Balham all those years ago is moving to Sydney, and will let his Islington flat to me for a nominal rent. Ironically he is going there on my recommendation, to start a new life after switching jobs from motorcycle couriering to computer programming.

And the company I now officially work for is changing address too. A merger has been announced, and we are going to use the sister company's offices rather than our own; we are moving to Soho.

My childhood is full of nostalgic memories of the West End. My father would often drive into town and park just off Leicester Square, while we went to see the latest big release at the Odeon, usually a James Bond film, in the days when traffic still circled the square. As a teenager, I bought clothes in Carnaby Street, found my first drum kit in a shop in Wardour Street, and saw my first soft porn film in one of the flea pit cinemas on Brewer Street. Needless to say, it's the unique atmosphere of this part of town that I remember so fondly, not the plot details of 'Confessions of a window cleaner'. And now that I am here, it feels like something of a sentimental return; I can't really imagine anywhere better to go to work.

Soon I get the salary rise that's due to me, and have money to spend. It feels good. I can now afford to buy rounds in our local, the Crown And Two Chairmen on Dean Street, even buy myself a video recorder. Summer is here, and 'Jurassic Park' has just hit the cinemas, raising the art of computer graphics to a new level. I feel lucky to be part of the same business; London has a long way to go before we catch up with the innovations going on in California, but I am now part of a cottage industry that is growing fast. Rather than animating dinosaurs, however, my job is to create tumbling logos for commercials and idents. It's not really art as I imagined it. One such project is a commercial for a carpet warehouse who want to advertise a cut-price sale; I make a 3D planet covered with one of their finest Axminsters, then roll out each different carpet like Saturn's rings around its orbit, revealing the sale price of each as the camera tracks over them. In the background, miniature rolled up carpets spin and sparkle like tiny stars. The name of the company is of course Carpet World; it's an extraordinarily tasteless piece of work, by far the most garish I will ever do.

At the other end of the scale, I get to work on something a bit closer to my heart. A satellite company requires a new title sequence for its football broadcast of the FA Cup. The brief is to recreate a model of the FA Cup and the twin towers of Wembley in 3D, reflecting archive footage of famous cup moments into the trophy while the camera pulls back to reveal the stadium. To model the stadium is straightforward, as we are easily able to source stock photos as reference. The trophy, however, needs to be photographed in close-up to get the detail required. Three of us are designated for this task: two from the 3D department, and a producer who will bring along a camera. Last years cup winners were Arsenal, and a visit to the stadium in Highbury is duly arranged ...

Despite being a Spurs fan, a tour of Highbury with the red carpet rolled out is something of a treat; we are proudly walked around the pitch and the back room offices by the club executives, before finally heading off to the trophy room. There, in a glass cabinet, sits the FA Cup - the fourth version of the silver trophy, commissioned only recently when the third was retired due to wear and tear. I can't resist holding it for a few minutes, both hands raising it aloft like the captain of a winning team, before I have to place it on a plinth to photograph. Then, as we circle the cup reverently with the Arsenal executives looking on, our producer steps up to take the pictures.

The camera, though, issues a disappointing 'thup' sound, not the anticipated 'ker-chick'. Another attempt is quickly made, but still the same dull thud. An embarrassed silence soon permeates the room. The camera is given several violent shakes, then a few thumps of the fist, an instant fix desperately willed on by everyone in the room ... but it's no good, the camera is jammed. And now, one by one, the executives slowly drift away, leaving us with only the janitor, who quietly replaces the cup in its case ...

The title sequence turns out well in the end. The cup was photographed the next day, and the result after four weeks is the first piece of work I feel genuine pride for. My professional life is beginning to bring me considerable satisfaction, and with the territory comes a social life too. Just outside our office doors, easily accessible after work, is London's entertainment district: pubs, cinemas, restaurants and nightclubs. Conveniently, there are no suits worn in our workplace, and we are already dressed for a night out. Going back to work drunk, however, is a common pitfall. After a heavy drinking session late one night, I find myself locked in at the office, having entered with a security card but unable to leave through a securely locked front door. I manage to find my way out of the back onto a fire escape, then drop fifteen feet, like a cat burglar, into a private courtyard. It leads into an underground garage that luckily has its shutter door open ten inches at the bottom, just enough for me to crawl under; a jump over an iron spike fence takes me back onto the street. Then, after a slow thirty-eight bus ride home, I fumble for my keys at the door. They're not there; I must have left them at the office. Still intoxicated, a marathon round trip ensues, completing the same assault course out of the back of the office, this time with my keys. It's not until the following week that I see, carefully hidden behind a column near the front door, a friendly green button with the words "Push to Exit" written helpfully on it ...

After only six months in the industry my salary gets another rise when the company gets bought out by a wealthy investor, and for the first time in my life I can afford not to think about money any more. Yet now that I have reached this position, it's odd to look back at why I took this path. Bella is long gone, and it's far too late for me to help Jamila now. The latest letter from her is the most tragic yet - she has been in prison again, six months this time, and when she was released, there was no sign of Otto anywhere. He was taken away at the beginning of her term, and the police will not reveal his whereabouts. She is now desperately searching every orphanage in Mombasa. I try to imagine how I could help if I flew out there, but I convince myself there is nothing I could do. And after a year of pushing those emotions to the back of my mind, the fear of sinking back into the futility of that relationship is too much to bear. I continue to write to her nevertheless, my letters always honest and pragmatic, but the advice as ever goes unheeded ...

And as time goes by, although I am content with the new life I'm leading, I occasionally miss the companionship of my travelling days. I've made friends through work, but nothing like the closeness I would get when meeting someone on the road, living out of each other's pockets. Perhaps it's the unspoken rivalry in the workplace that inhibits too much openness, but we also lack something of a free spirit amongst us. Everyone, including me, takes themselves a little too seriously; it's part of the illusion of appearing professional. Responsibility, it seems to me, is a rather sobering experience.

I'm still seeing Stacey from time to time though, when I need a bit of craziness to balance my life. We go out drinking in Hackney, where she tells me she's banned from a couple of the local pubs, one for doing cartwheels on the bar:

"My friend bet me I couldn't do it," she says in justification, "and I didn't fall off ..."

She's not working, so I offer to take her for a weeks holiday in the South of France. As part of our nostalgia for a carefree existence, we travel without luggage, each of us taking just one change of clothes in a small knapsack. Every day we walk from one village to the next, staying in small bed and breakfasts where we wash our clothes in the sink. It's a beautiful part of the world, and one of my most enjoyable holidays ever; I feel like I could just keep on walking ...

Over the next two years, my life settles into a steady routine, although it might otherwise be described as a rut. My career, despite a promising start, begins to stagnate. The company is lagging behind its competitors with the quality of its work, and as a result, my showreel is not good enough to change jobs. Interviews with rival outfits only serve to highlight my deficiencies, and I am left to wonder how I can manoeuvre my way out of this predicament.

On a personal level though, things are going much better. As if in counter balance to my professional gloom, the genial girl who helped me get my first job is now my girlfriend, and we regularly travel abroad together as a couple, a pleasure I rarely experienced as a traveller. Suzi is now working for a film company, where on a much smaller scale the same kind of innovative work is being done as it is in California. This film work, however, requires a higher resolution than video and takes much longer to process, and I am already frustrated at the speed of my task. A typical day for me would require waiting two hours or more to render one frame of animation, whereupon if something goes wrong, I have to start all over again. Working through the night is not uncommon when a deadline looms, and I frequently sleep on the couch at work. But there is a new technology that has just arrived in the building. This latest piece of kit runs on a computer the size of a large fridge-freezer and costs close to a million pounds; and for that exorbitant price, it brings some of the simpler 3D tasks into almost realtime. It's called a Flame.

Sensing an opportunity to escape from my rut, I train on the Flame when it's free in the evenings, and in the day I write software plug-ins to add new functionality. One such plug-in saves us weeks of work on a Coca Cola commercial we are working on; suitably impressed, the management give me formal training and promote me to a new position as a Flame artist. My salary gets a hike once again, but more importantly, my career is back on track ...

Unfortunately though, with more money comes more responsibility. Rather than working quietly in an office waiting for an image to slowly render in front of me, I now have clients sat behind me watching me as I work - and they are paying six hundred pounds an hour for the privilege. The pressure is enormous, and my role has changed very quickly from back room geek to a kind of performing monkey. Even the room I work in is intimidating; interior designed in a modern art deco style, there are three sofas, four TV monitors, and in front of me a switchboard jammed with buttons and controls. A microphone puts me through to the machine room where tapes are changed rapidly at my request, and a switch operates a motorised blind which rolls up and down the window like a garage door. It looks like the bridge of the Starship Enterprise, and I follow up my commands to the tape room with a Captain Picardesque: "Make it so."

At this point I am wondering if this is as far as I want to go in this industry. After all, I am earning good money and have a skill that's in high demand. I see a future filled with dollar signs and 'sorted for life' written all over it - perhaps I can even retire early. It is of course a blindingly short-sighted vision. And it's not very long at all before everything changes once again ...

back on the conveyor

How clear it is now, how easy to see, now that light is cast on this talent unleashed!

See how simple it is to step on to the conveyor, and see how far and how speedily it goes!

See how those naysayers were right pouring scorn; this waster, this layabout with nothing to give, is now in a place where he always belonged.

Was there so much to fear, so much to lose, from taking this step during all of these years?

No, there is but one question that remains: how did it take so interminably long?

Yet how can we know which is better or worse, when time puts its stamp on each different course, with never the same result gained twice?

All we can say is that both courses flowed, rather than one or the other: a journey abroad and a journey at home.

And is it not richer to do both, than to do one at the other's expense: the adventure and adversity of one, the comfort, the esteem of the other?

What kind of life should be chosen? Which course should be run?

I propose both; and each in it's own good time ...

25. paradise revisited

Of all the places in the world, there is probably only one that could tempt me away from London. Although most aspiring CG artists are heading to San Francisco or Los Angeles for higher salaries and better career opportunities, I am more interested in the lifestyle and aesthetics of another faraway city, one that I've had the good fortune to experience already: Sydney.

In another chain of serendipitous events, a film is shooting down under and a new company is being formed to do the visual effects. Suzi has been invited to join and has already gone out. Reluctant to squander my new found role as a Flame artist, I resist for a few months, until a call from Suzi changes my mind. Lured by the chance to revisit my favourite city in the world and be reunited with my girlfriend, I happily relent. Although the offer of employment is for two days a week only, with no promises of an extension, it's a gamble I'm prepared to take.

At my leaving party in London, the company announce that they have made me a showreel to take with me to Australia; a producer hits the play button, and it starts up on a large screen above the bar. Set to the gaudy music 'Sign of the swinging cymbal', the Carpet World commercial plays in an endless loop, back and forth, zooming in, zooming out, then dividing like cells into a huge mosaic, over and over and over again ...

On my return to Sydney after an eight year absence, it would be fair to say that the biggest thing that's changed is myself. Yes, the monorail is now operational, and Darling Harbour - a massive new development with an aquarium and Imax theatre - has been built; but the essential beauty of the harbour is unchanged. And instead of living in the travellers Mecca of Kings Cross, I now reside in the wealthy middle class suburb of Kirribilli, with its views across the bay to the business district and opera house. From the balcony of Suzi's flat, we can see the coat hanger bridge and hear the constant rumble of traffic heading into the city.

Our daily commute is to the nearby suburb of Crows Nest, a centre for media and broadcast, and in the very first week the risk I took in coming here pays off: the two-day-week never materialises - money has somehow been found in the budget to keep me on full time. And the job is hugely enjoyable. I soon find that working in film is slower yet more rewarding than commercials, and where before I was surrounded by advertising agency types, now there is only an occasional relaxed visit from the film's director. After two weeks, I get my first 'final', a finished shot approved by the director for the film, and I am very quickly back in the swing ...

Life in Sydney as a professional is just as good as it was when I was a traveller, with the sun out most days, and the beaches close enough to get to in twenty minutes or so. But my lifestyle has changed, and now I find myself experiencing a different side to the city. As half of a professional couple, restaurants are now my staple rather than the sandwich bars of old, and here in Sydney they are exceptionally good and cheap. Much of the innovative cuisine is called fusion - an east-west mix of sweet and savoury tastes - and in most restaurants you bring your own beer or wine from the bottle shop on the corner. I also discover sushi for the first time, and concoct my own dish at the fish market by buying salmon sashimi at one counter, then chips at another; with wasabi and soy sauce replacing salt and vinegar, it shocks me to say that no-one else seems to have thought of this obvious refashioning of the 'fish and chips' classic.

My leisure pursuits too have changed. From the crazy holes of the Amstelpark mini golf in Amsterdam, I now step up to the big game. In the North Shore of Sydney there are many affordable golf courses open to the public, most of them in beautiful locations. Suzi and I play with another English couple, taking out chunks of grass here and there in a frustrating attempt to hit the ball around the course. It's a ridiculously difficult sport, but fun nevertheless, and we are often joined by kangaroos as we curse our way around the long nine holes searching for lost balls.

We buy ourselves a car, an open top beetle with fat wheels like a beach buggy, and drive out to the national parks that surround the city - Kuringai to the north, Royal to the south, and the Blue Mountains to the west. And soon we get the chance to make our stay even more comfortable; the lease is up on our apartment, and we find a new one round the corner with a view of Neutral Bay from every window and a communal swimming pool in its shorefront gardens. The rent is cheap, less than a rundown flat in London, yet it feels like living in a holiday apartment. There are yachts moored close by in the bay, and the tinkle of their bells as they rock back and forth creates the soothing sound of distant wind chimes. In the day we get visits from rainbow lorikeets, who land noisily on our veranda asking for food, and at dusk the sky darkens with the silent silhouettes of giant fruit bats on their daily migration across the bay to feed; when the moon is out, it's like a scene from a vampire movie.

But being Australia, there are creatures that abound who are far less agreeable than these. The Huntsman spider, though less venomous than either the Funnel Web or Redback, is, however, extremely large. And when I close the bedroom door to find a spider as big as my hand staring at me, it's a massive shock; the sheer size of it registers long before any logical reasoning can kick in; dangerous or not, I jump completely out of my skin. Similarly, as I drive to work one day, a Huntsman suddenly appears on my windscreen, having woken from its slumber in my engine compartment; zigzagging along the road with wipers flashing furiously, I nearly cause an accident. I am later told that these spiders like to come inside for the rainy months, and it's certainly true that we have recently seen a deluge. There is an upside to this new infestation, however; soon it will be spring, and with that change of season comes not only the good weather, but also the end of my first film project ...

When the film is finished we decide to stay on in Sydney. There is no extra work guaranteed yet, but we are payed a retainer while we bid for new projects. This new arrangement allows us more time off to enjoy Australia, and we make several trips around New South Wales, as well as to Melbourne and the Great Barrier Reef. Swimming with sharks provides a highlight, though admittedly they are of the small reef variety and hardly dangerous at all; through the magnification of an underwater mask, however, five feet can easily look like eight ...

And although I am enjoying this country enormously, I find myself once again socialising with my compatriots far more than the locals. An element of this is pure laziness, but the culture difference, while small, is significant nonetheless. From my side the constant Aussie undertone of friendly rivalry is often an irritation, and from theirs I sense an intolerance to any hint of negativity or criticism. The 'whinging pom' jibe that's aimed at every Englishman suggests as much, but often that attitude prevents any serious conversation, especially for a cynic like myself. On one occasion, I am comparing careers with a lawyer who is about to retire and go travelling. I list all the aspects I dislike about my job and would like to change, hoping to open up a discussion.

"Why don't you just kill yourself?" he responds, and walks off. He wasn't joking.

After almost three months without work, one of the projects we are bidding on is confirmed; it's a science fiction film similar to the one we've just completed, and our previous work has helped secure the project. My boss Don, though, has a dilemma. He is stepping up to a more managerial role and needs to recruit someone to replace him as supervisor for the project. The company has interviewed two or three people, but none have worked out for various reasons. One day during a meeting, he asks the room casually:

"Look, if I can't find a supervisor, does anyone here think they can do it?"

I immediately stick my hand up. "I'll do it," I say confidently.

I look quickly around the room - there are no more hands up. Having supervised a sequence on the previous film, I am one of the more likely choices, but it had never occurred to me that there would be an opportunity like this. Suzi too would make a good candidate, though she's not in this particular meeting. Nevertheless, it's pure conjecture at this point, with more interviews scheduled for external candidates, and only an off-the-cuff comment by Don to suggest otherwise.

Two weeks later, however, I get a call at home. It's Don:

"If you still want to do it, there's a lunch arranged tomorrow with the client. I want to introduce you as our supervisor. What do you think?"

We talk for a while about my inexperience and how we might compensate for it, but there is no way I will let this one go; I want to step up. Sure enough, the next day I am introduced to the client as promised ...

The brand new Fox Studios are beginning to attract a few Hollywood films to Sydney, partly through tax breaks and partly through a favourable exchange rate. The directors in this case are also keen to make their film away from the prying eyes of the studio in Los Angeles, who have a propensity to interfere with the creative process. For me, it's a baptism of fire, as this will be my first film shoot to attend. Fortunately though, I will not be alone; there are three companies doing the visual effects work on the film, each with its own supervisor, and these three answer to one overall production supervisor from the U.S. who is essentially my client.

The experience on set turns out to be a combination of intense boredom and insane activity. Most of the day is spent in preparation and waiting, which for visual effects means setting up green-screens, testing wire rigs, and placing tracking markers in the appropriate place; but when the cameras roll, the problems come thick and fast, and decisions need to be made quickly. It's like waiting all day for a bus that will leave you standing unless you're ready to run and jump on board at the precise moment it zooms past - mostly uneventful, but never relaxing.

Nevertheless, the shoot takes me all around Sydney to a number of diverse but interesting locations. Some of it is filmed from the rooftops of the business district, and at one point I have the task of placing tracking markers halfway down the side of a skyscraper. Hanging onto a window cleaning platform lowered precariously from a crane on the roof, I inspect the cables carefully for signs of wear and tear, imagining how I would cling on if one of them breaks. Several months later, these bright green squares will still be visible from the other side of the bay, long forgotten and threatening to become a permanent fixture on the Sydney skyline. A similar location on the schedule is a restaurant on the forty-second floor of another downtown high-rise building. On a break, the crew recommend that I try out the toilets. The urinals are strategically mounted on the floor-to-ceiling glass of the building facade, with extensive views over the harbour and beyond; it's one of the best places to piss in the world.

And when the shoot is over, the producers organise an extravagant wrap party. For one night only, the abandoned Luna Park on the North Shore of the Sydney Harbour Bridge is reopened for our sole benefit. The lights are switched on, the bumper cars reignited and the flying teacups relaunched; and with its teeth lit up for the first time in years, the huge smiley face that adorns the neglected entrance doesn't look quite so sad any more.

After that milestone celebration, the nine month post-production phase becomes somewhat tortuous for me. First I fall out with Suzi after blazing rows both at home and at work; I am effectively her boss now, and although I try hard to tread carefully and do the job as best I can, it's never quite good enough. She moves out of the apartment, but somehow we manage to remain good friends.

Soon after that, Don has his eye on my job. With no more work coming in, his managerial position has become a little pointless, and he colludes with one of the film's producers to stage a coup against me. The producer, known amongst us as the 'smiling assassin', wants to make his mark and seize more control of the creative process; he asks Don to do our next company presentation, instead of me. But it's an ill conceived plan; the directors have not been consulted. Outraged, they demand that I am reinstated in the role. And although it's something of a triumph for me on this occasion, I have at the same time made a long-term enemy of my boss ...

Our relationship quickly deteriorates over the following weeks, and we soon reach something of an impasse. Both of us are headstrong; Don, in his previous incarnation as an editor, famously threw a tape at a client in frustration, and I too can quickly see red at a perceived injustice. A few skirmishes ensue, and by the end of the project he is crossing the street to avoid me.

In the background to all this, the work itself is going reasonably well. The creative collusion with the directors is particularly good; invited into the inner circle from early on, they have been inclusive in every part of the process. And when a first cut is ready for viewing, it's the visual effects supervisors who are exclusively invited to the screening; afterwards they ask us each in turn our opinion of the film. The producers, however, wait nervously outside, asking for scraps of information as we file out of the room. Although I recognise this moment as something special, it will be another fourteen years before I get the same privilege again ...

And so, as the project comes to an end, I can sense the sands of time running out for me in Sydney. In an ideal world, Don would have walked from the company and I would have been able to carry on; instead it's me who has to walk, and I am faced with only one alternative source of employment in the city. My interview with the rival goes well enough, but unfortunately they can only offer me a position in commercials, a backwards step for me. I politely decline, and head back to Kirribilli to pack my bags once again. In my second chance to make it in the city of my dreams, I have lasted only two films, two years and two months precisely ...

26. the unexpected call

No sooner have I arrived back in London than I receive an invitation to the film's premiere in Los Angeles. Since I have already left the company, I pay for the trip myself, staying in a cheap hotel near the sea front in Santa Monica. It's my third visit to LA now, following two trips from Sydney for client presentations, and it means I have accidentally circumnavigated the globe in the last three weeks - from LA to Sydney to London to LA. The film goes down remarkably well, with boisterous applause throughout the screening, and I manage to get into the post premiere party at some fashionable venue on Sunset Boulevard afterwards. With great reviews the next day, there is a sense of closure to the twelve months I spent on the project, and I return home happy to have made a contribution.

But despite the sudden end to my Australian dream, returning to London is far from disappointing. I find myself looking forward to the social life of Soho and my reacquaintance with old friends. And I also return with a new certainty in my career; I'm enjoying the work and want to continue along this path. There is something about leaving your mark on a film for posterity, however small the contribution, that lifts the experience above the day to day humdrum. There are as many as five companies in London that I can get film work, and after interest from three of them, I take up one of the offers on a freelance contract.

This new feeling of security also makes me want to put down roots. I have saved enough money now to put down a deposit on a flat, and after a brief search I come across the ideal place; set in a converted Georgian house down a quiet alleyway in Soho, the flat is decked out with wooden floors, ultra-modern kitchen, and a lift that opens straight into the hallway. It's a massive milestone in my life, and a crazy amount of money to part with; when I imagine lining up a hundred perfectly decent second hand cars for the same price, my mind boggles at the insanity of it. But I go ahead nevertheless; and now, at the tender age of thirty-seven, I can say for the first time in my life that I'm a man of property ...

Soon I decamp to a new company where many of my ex-colleagues from Sydney are now working; Don's company had gone bust soon after I left Australia, and a number of the staff, including Suzi, have resurfaced here. It was the first digital film facility in London and has all the eccentricity you might expect from a group of early innovators; amongst my colleagues are a part time dairy farmer, an installation artist who sells his work to pop stars, and an engineer who builds stress test machines for the Scientology cult.

We are working on a top secret project on the uppermost floor of a four storey building, in a small, cramped room with 'Area 51' scrawled on the door. The work involves creating computer generated naked women to stand strategically in front of copulating couples with their backs to camera, thus hiding the lurid action; we are sworn to secrecy because the film's producers don't want to admit to any digital interference with their film, yet they need to cover up some of the action to get past the censors. In some ways it's a thankless task: we will get no credits on the film, nor publicity for our work. On the other hand, if nobody notices, then our job is well done. And being the professionals that we are, we need to get some good reference material for the women. A test shoot is arranged in a nearby studio with models posing for us naked; although the shoot is overseen by Suzi, I am reluctantly dragged along as the cameraman ...

When the project is finished, we get some welcome downtime. Although the company is doing several film projects at once, none of them have reached that stressful deadline stage yet. Still somewhat secluded on the top floor, we invent a new game of keepy-uppy using office chairs and a small plushy football about five inches across. The rules are simple: participants need to remain seated, using only the chair wheels to move around the room, and the ball must be kept in the air for as long as possible. Bouncing off desks and computer monitors is allowed, but when it hits the floor or stops moving, the rally is over. The number of kicks are recorded and the highest score is the one to beat. Like the bed tennis Kurt and I played in Bangkok, we frequently collapse in hysterics as we approach a new world record, especially when reaching the important milestones of fifty or a hundred. When the ball sometimes escapes out of an open window, the runners downstairs are called to fetch the ball from the street; and when a producer enters the room, all chairs are immediately spun back into their work positions as the ball drops silently to the floor ...

It's the most relaxed I've been for years, and the laughter is a welcome visitor into my life. My local pub has now changed to the George in Wardour Street, where every Friday a group of us gather for a drink. Often we all crowd into the Maharani on Berwick Street afterwards, where tables are rapidly joined together to cater to our party. The pièce de résistance of this particular Indian restaurant is a moving picture that takes pride of place on the end wall; lit from behind, the illusion of water cascading gently down a waterfall is created by its moving parts. Seen through drunken eyes, it's something of a masterpiece. On a few occasions I offer to buy it from them, but curiously they won't sell at any price; as a result, this captivating waterfall soon becomes something of an enigma amongst us - it's the picture that can't be bought.

And times have changed since I was last in Soho. With the recent advent of mobile phones, evenings out are much easier to extend into the night; a quick text soon reveals which venue everyone has moved to, or where a party's being held. If all options are exhausted, most of us have a cheap subscription to the Arts Club, a basement bar that sells beer long into the night to the nostalgic sounds of seventies disco. And in the early hours when I've had enough, I can conveniently crash into a bed that awaits only minutes away in my Dean Street flat. In the mornings the streets are quiet once again, and I awake slowly to the peaceful sounds of a small village, as Soho drags itself wearily out of bed for another day ...

In the midst of this happy yet somewhat debauched existence, a shock is awaiting me. As the old millennium comes to a close and a new one begins, there are forces at work that will conspire to change my world. The call, when it comes, is out of the blue:

"Is that Jon?"

It's the voice of the American supervisor from the film I worked on in Sydney. A little confused, I respond in the affirmative.

"I'm here with the directors actually. We've got some news we'd like to tell you. Are you sitting down?"

"Er ... yes."

"You've been chosen as one of the four we're putting forward to the academy for this year's awards."

I'm completely taken aback. The only clue I had to this was when my producer in Sydney told me that my credit on the film was in a nominatable role. I had since forgotten all about it.

"You need to prepare some text about the work you did. Next week we'll meet in LA for the bake-off presentation. We're one of seven films on the short list for visual effects; the academy picks three for a nomination and we're in with a good shot."

In no time at all I am back in Los Angeles once again. It seems so sudden, but the craziness is only just beginning ...

Two weeks after I return from the bake-off, the nominations are announced, and astonishingly I am on the list. It's a surreal moment as I now break the news to family and friends:

"Er ... you'll never guess what ... I've just been nominated for an Oscar."

The words sound ludicrous coming from my lips, and for a while I feel like I've stepped into a different world. I've never had much interest in the Oscar ceremony before, but I'm well aware of the prestige and recognition it gets from its role in Hollywood celebrity culture. At the very least it's going to be an interesting ride. Variety magazine has given us a fifty percent chance of winning, and I picture an imaginary coin being tossed somewhere to settle my fate.

But as the days progress towards the ceremony, there are more practical concerns. Although thankfully the studio have agreed to pay for my trip to LA, I am missing two crucial accompaniments for an event as important as this: a suit, which I've never owned, and a partner, which I don't currently have. The former is fairly easy to solve, although not without a short but unfamiliar period of fashion anguish. The latter, er, is much harder. It occurs to me that I could proposition a the street in an impulsive romantic gesture, like a once-in-alifetime blind date - but I quickly decide against it. Instead I offer to take Suzi first, who declines, then Christina, a producer from the film, who accepts. Everything is lined up now: the Ted Baker suit, the glamorous partner, the first class tickets, and the black stretch limo. All that remains is to subject myself to that heart-stopping moment ...

It's easy for the nerves to get hold of you in a situation like this. As the show gets underway, I can see that there is about an hour in the schedule before our category comes up, and it's impossible to enjoy anything that's going on in the meantime. My breathing is shallow, and my heart starts pounding heavily. What if I have to go up on stage with half a billion people watching? And as my head struggles to contain a body in full panic mode, I slowly begin to realise something. Surely it would be better to win and go through this small inconvenience? Imagine getting so close and losing? There will never be another chance like this.

At once, my body settles down, the heartbeat returns to normal, and I take a long deep breath ...

"And the Oscar goes to ..." Arnie is on stage now, tearing open the envelope.

"John ..." The first word that comes out of his mouth is not the name of our film. My heart skips a beat - we lost. But then the words start forming the name of people, not a film, and soon they become my colleague's names, then mine.

Actually, we've won.

I walk behind the others onto the stage in a daze, as Arnie shakes my hand saying, "Yah .. really great .." in that famous Austrian drawl. The Oscar is heavy, and instinctively I hold it out in front of me for balance; as the American supervisor makes his long speech, I realise I'm holding it like a massive dildo, rooted in my crotch and aimed squarely at the audience. But I don't care, I am transfixed by the moment; and rather than change my posture in an admission of guilt, I stay phallically poised until the music drowns him out and we are led off the back of the stage for the awaiting press.

In truth, I am relieved not to have made a speech at the Oscars; my fear of public speaking is based soundly on my lack of experience, and in any case my chance will soon come at the BAFTAs, where we are destined to win again in a few weeks time. Now though, there is an evening of celebration to look forward to. After dining in the banqueting hall, we pile into our limo with the sound guys and head out into the night; they also won Oscars, and as we approach a roadblock to the Vanity Fair party, we brandish them through the sunroof like golden tickets to the ball. We are waved through immediately, and quickly disembark to spend the rest of the evening celebrity spotting. But rather than just gawk, Christina, a little worse for wear, attempts to strike up a friendly conversation here and there. The compère of the show, a well known comedian, is asked:

"That was amazing, did you have a script or was it spontaneous?"

"What do you think?" comes the icy reply.

"Weren't you nervous?" she carries on recklessly.

"Of course," he intones, equally stonily. Needless to say, the conversation dies soon afterwards.

But it's a euphoric occasion for us nevertheless, and nothing can dampen our spirit. The only disappointment is that the night ends too soon, when LA shuts down at two in the morning, and I return reluctantly to my hotel. I am still buzzing so much that it's impossible to sleep.

The Oscar has an especially big cachet in Los Angeles, and as I take my cab to the airport the next day, the driver asks me to hold it up for him to see. A girl pulls up in a car alongside and smiles at me through her open window in appreciation.

"Man, why don't you stay in LA and get laid? Can't you see the reaction you're getting?" he says.

But I've made a promise to return to work for a looming deadline, and I'm anxious to get back anyway. On the plane, the hostess brings me a DVD of the film to sign for her son, after recognising me from the flight ⸻lishly I sign the disk without a personal message, unaware of the ⸻e hostess looks disappointed but doesn't protest. Later, she ⸻t from the captain to see my Oscar, but annoyingly the invitation doesn't extend to me; perhaps in retribution, it's taken into the cockpit unaccompanied ...

And back in London, there are similar requests for public inspection. Out of all of my family, my brother has the most appreciative reaction, describing how he stayed up all night to watch the show and almost fell off his chair when I won; he books a table at the Ivy at the last minute, and the Oscar takes pride of place in the centre of table. It generates more interest than all the dining celebrities combined. The maitre d' says to me quietly on leaving: "Come back anytime, sir," though it's not an offer I am likely to take up.

There is, however, one place where I am determined to show it off more than any other. After a particularly rowdy Friday night, I collect the Oscar from my flat and take it to the Maharani wrapped in a plastic bag, where about fifteen of us have assembled for a late night curry. After plonking it on the table, the Indian waiters are nonplussed:

"Yes sir ... er ... very nice sir. What is it?" they ask politely.

"It doesn't matter," I reply, thinking an explanation is perhaps beside the point. After years of trying, nothing, it seems, will ever upstage that magnificent waterfall.

27. old chinese saying: be careful what you wish

It would be wrong to suggest that the adrenaline of this adventure did not persist, or that the benefits of the win did not unfold in due course. Soon there are sequels planned for the film, and a chance arises for me to work on them. Alongside that, a strange excursion manifests itself: I am flown to Hawaii first class to visit a company who are bidding to work on the sequels, but the Japanese owners are suddenly taken ill with flu. I stay in a five star hotel on the beach for four days, swimming and snorkelling, waiting for them to recover. Although I get a tour of the company and a few evenings out with friends, they never turn up, and I head back home never to hear from them again.

Back in London, the reaction is mixed. A letter from Downing Street contains a handwritten note from Tony Blair saying he enjoyed the film, and similar congratulatory letters arrive from the British Film Commission, the Culture Minister and the British Film Office. However, the company I work for shows little interest in publicising the win as the work was done elsewhere, and with four other supervisors in the office ostensibly my senior, a few noses are distinctly out of joint. In some ways this win has come too early; being only my second film, it's arrived before I've had time to get enough experience under my belt, and while this event will come to define me in many people's eyes, right now it feels like an ill-fitting suit.

Nevertheless, there's no doubt that the future looks good for me professionally; it's the personal side that's more worrying. The reaction amongst colleagues and friends to my success is wildly fluctuating; there are those that make fun in a nice way, and those that make fun with an underlying resentment; some are openly happy for me, and some are conspicuously silent. A drunken rant occasionally surfaces as to my undeserved fate, and a polite agreement by me does little to curtail the diatribe.

My life, it's true, has been changed by one long chain of good luck, not least being in the right continent at the right time, but there was perhaps one significant intervention by me nonetheless - that I took advantage when the opportunity arose. Unfortunately, this can be viewed from the outside in two very different ways: as a talent destined to succeed, or as a completely lucky bastard ...

And as I embark now on a new quest to build on this success and provide a home for a family one day, I must leave this debate behind. I can only make the most of my good fortune while it's here and take each opportunity as it comes. As the distance of old friendships begins to grow, I remind myself of the long journey that brought me here, from busker and shit shoveller to delivery driver and traveller, and the one important lesson I must take from those times - that there will always be something new and unexpected waiting patiently for me around the bend ...

Although my nomadic days have long since passed, I am still revisited by the memories of that period. Occasionally a smell or a vision will take me back to a place that I have been, a street or a bar in some faraway country. In an instant I am there, and for a few seconds I am lost in thought as I try to identify the accompanying emotion; it's a pleasant and reassuring feeling, a simple nostalgia for the past. At other times though, the memories are more insidious; for on these rare occasions, they visit me while I sleep.

In my childhood, a classic anxiety dream would often reoccur: I am trying to run but going nowhere, floating off the ground whenever I try to propel myself forwards, like a race staged in zero gravity while all around me are rooted firmly to the ground. After my student days, I acquired a new one to accompany this: the dream of the unfathomable exam paper. And now I have two more. The first involves packing bags: in this dream, there is never enough room in my suitcase for all the items I need to take with me; soon I look around me to see stereos, bicycles, all kinds of impossible objects mounting up that cannot possibly fit inside. Either a plane is leaving shortly, or a train will stop only briefly while I desperately try to load all my possessions on board. It appears to be a hangup from the days when every morning I would pack my bag for the next hotel, careful to leave nothing behind. Possessions seemed to take on a greater meaning in those days, when money was short; now it's odd to awake from that dream still feeling the fear that has long since passed.

The second type of anxiety dream is even more disconcerting, no doubt triggered by the poor sanitation I encountered regularly on my travels. Here, I find myself unable to find a suitable toilet in time, and being forced to defecate in a public place. I take care not to be noticed, but soon the situation degenerates. Shit gets stuck to my shoe or a piece of clothing, or someone walks past and asks me what I'm doing. Sometimes it's an especially inappropriate place to go, like a wastepaper bin in someone's living room; never is there any toilet paper, and always I am discovered. Fortunately the situation is unfailingly resolved when finally, and blissfully, I wake up to find myself and my bed mercifully clean and dry.

That is, so far.

who am I?

Who is this voice of reason, this confidante to author and reader alike, this arbitrator of prosecution and defence?
I'm sure you have guessed: we are one and the same.
For I am the older and wiser he, and he the younger impetuous I.
And fifteen years hence, one will merge seamlessly into the other.

Then who am I to judge, you may well ask?
For what person judges themselves as harshly as they judge others? What person can claim immunity to hypocrisy?
Perhaps none, and certainly not I.
And that is why, at the end of this journey, you must be the judge ...

For the rants and the diatribes we have heard so noisily from the prosecution are not my own, but the constant sound of those old establishment mores that echo to this day from all about us: the pressure to conform, the need to hold on tightly to the conveyor belt for fear of falling off. These were the voices in my head.

But what then drives a man to step off, to rebel against the order of things?
Perhaps the fear of that very thing he is urged to pursue - the conveyor belt itself.
For viewed from aboard it is a comfortable ride indeed; it carries you forward and all of those around you in harmonious step.
But from the outside, those very same people seem like rats in a maze, lured by rewards of material wealth in an endless cycle of unquenchable desire.

And what little choice these rebels face!
How hard to exist outside of a world hellbent on hurtling blindly forth into an unknown future!
For the most, it will reel them in or run them down.

But that this world now has me firmly in its hold cannot be denied.
The truth is out: I have succumbed to the pressure; I have returned to the
fold.
And it is far easier to tolerate through mellower, less idealistic eyes.

There can be no regrets, save a precious few; and that small group must
be respectfully reserved for those good friends I have sadly left behind ...

Kurt

Although I lost touch with Kurt in 1994, I found him again in 2010 thanks to that new invention, the internet. He was living happily in Holland with his long term girlfriend, two dogs and a horse, and occasionally sailing the Atlantic for recreation. For years he thought that "some hotshot from Hollywood" he saw on the internet with my name couldn't possibly be me.

Stacey

I last visited Stacey in 2004, when she was living alone in Ashford and struggling with psychosis, a debilitating mental illness. She was endeavouring to start a career as a writer.

Yishai

I last talked to Yishai by phone in 1994. Strange to my ears, he spoke in broken English, and was making plans to live in Tokyo with his Japanese girlfriend. Although I've called many times since, he never picked up the phone again.

Jamila

Jamila's letters stopped abruptly in 1994, the last one confirming that she still hadn't found her son Otto. In 2014 I managed to renew contact with a mutual friend in Nairobi; it turned out that she too had not heard from Jamila since 1994. She appears to have vanished off the face of the earth.

For a photographic accompaniment,
and further information, please visit:

www.jonthum.com

6265804R00143

Printed in Germany
by Amazon Distribution
GmbH, Leipzig